# Table of contents

## Preface

The decision to delve into a case study on Coca-Cola was driven by a profound curiosity about what propels a global icon to enduring success amidst a dynamically evolving market landscape. Coca-Cola, an emblematic brand that spans continents and cultures, has not only stood the test of time but has consistently set benchmarks in the realm of consumer goods and marketing strategies.

This case study aims to unravel the underlying principles and strategies that have fortified Coca-Cola's position as a leader in the beverage industry. Through meticulous research and analysis, I seek to uncover the pivotal decisions, innovative campaigns, and adaptive measures that have shaped its trajectory from its humble beginnings to its current global stature.

Moreover, the allure of Coca-Cola lies not only in its commercial success but also in its cultural impact. From its inception in 1886 to its present-day operations, Coca-Cola has woven itself into the fabric of societies worldwide, becoming synonymous with shared moments of joy, celebration, and refreshment.

As I embarked on this journey of exploration, I was drawn to the multifaceted dimensions of Coca-Cola's story: the challenges it has overcome, the strategies it has employed, and the values it upholds. By examining these aspects, I aim to distill valuable insights that can inform and inspire both aspiring entrepreneurs and seasoned professionals navigating today's competitive business environment.

Ultimately, this case study is a testament to the enduring relevance and resilience of Coca-Cola as a brand that not only adapts to change but also drives it. It is my hope that readers will find within these pages not only a deeper understanding of Coca-Cola's journey but also actionable lessons that transcend industry boundaries.

In documenting the evolution of Coca-Cola, I am reminded of the profound impact that strategic vision, innovation, and a commitment to consumer satisfaction can have on shaping the destiny of a global powerhouse. This case study is my humble endeavor to illuminate these dynamics and contribute to the ongoing dialogue on what it takes to sustain leadership in an ever-evolving marketplace.

May this exploration into Coca-Cola's journey serve as both a tribute to its storied legacy and a source of inspiration for future generations of business leaders and enthusiasts alike.

## Disclaimer

This case study is a student-written project and is intended for educational purposes only. The content reflects the author's independent research and interpretation of the subject matter, and may not fully represent professional opinions, current industry standards, or real-life scenarios. All information presented is based on publicly available sources or hypothetical situations unless otherwise cited.

The findings, conclusions, and recommendations in this case study are those of the author(s) and do not necessarily reflect the views of any institution, organization, or external body. Any resemblance to actual persons or events is purely coincidental unless explicitly stated.

The case study should not be used as a substitute for professional advice. Neither the author(s) nor the institution assume any liability for actions taken based on the content herein.

<h1 align="center">Acknowledgement</h1>

Writing this case study on Coca-Cola has been a rewarding and insightful experience. The completion of this study would not have been possible without the support and guidance of several individuals and organizations. I would like to express my deepest gratitude to all those who have contributed to this endeavor.

First and foremost, I would like to thank Yashi Shukla ma'am, whose invaluable guidance, encouragement, and expertise have been instrumental throughout the entire process. Her constructive feedback and insightful suggestions have significantly enhanced the quality of this case study.

I am also immensely grateful to Gokul Prabhu sir for providing me with the necessary resources and a conducive environment to conduct this research. The access to extensive databases and research materials has been crucial in gathering the relevant information and data for this study.

I would like to extend my heartfelt appreciation to my colleagues and peers for their continuous support and encouragement. Their valuable discussions, inputs, and moral support have been a great source of motivation.

I am also thankful to my family and friends for their unwavering support and understanding throughout this journey. Their patience and encouragement have been my pillars of strength.

Lastly, I would like to acknowledge all the authors, researchers, and industry experts whose works have been referenced in this case study. Their research and insights have provided a strong foundation for this study.

This case study is a culmination of collective efforts and contributions from many individuals. I am deeply grateful to each one of you for your support, guidance, and encouragement.

Thank you.

**Introduction**

Coke, a soda that has been perpetuated over the years, across cultural and national boundaries, is more than just a carbonated beverage; it is a worldwide symbol of refreshment, happiness and togetherness. In 1886, Coca-Cola was born in Atlanta, Georgia and today it has become one of the most famous brands in the world. From simple fountain soda syrup, this path traveled through disappearance into pop culture – which shows exactly how appealing and well-marketed the product was.

In its essence, Coca-Cola embodies a fusion of flavors, trademarks and cultural meanings. The original recipe was initially developed by pharmacist John S. Pemberton as a sort of medication tonic promising to alleviate fatigue as well as headaches. Yet it was Asa Candler's idea after buying out Pemberton in 1888 that made Coca-Cola become an industry leader. Under Candler's direction Coca-Cola went from being a local remedy to a nationwide drink sold in bottles throughout America.

Coca-Cola's 20th-century marketing strategies were very important in shaping the company's identity and expanding its market. The brand's red-and-white icon, which came into existence in 1886, has almost never been changed, showing consistency and reliability. All over the world Coca Cola advertisements have been nothing but emotional and have always touched hearts of many people with its famous "I'd like to buy the world a coke" video and every Christmas' holiday season brings forth scenes of polar bears on TV courtesy of Coca Cola.

Apart from other factors that have contributed to making this company one of the best marketers of all times is its capacity to adapt to changing consumer tastes and market conditions. Diet Coke, fruit-flavored and caffeine-free versions as well as other types such as Coca-Cola Zero Sugar has been introduced by the firm at different times to serve customers with different preferences. This way, while evolving along with consumers' changing tastes and growing lifestyles, Coca-Cola has not lost sight of who it truly is.

This also involves some aspect related to society beyond just advertising: being socially responsible. The examples are numerous; beginning from sustainable development initiatives and culminating into community empowerment programs everybody can refer to Coca Cola as a perfect illustration of how business can change this planet for better.

The presence of Coca-Cola is felt throughout the world with operations in over 200 countries and territories. The company's ability to develop a local brand while worldwide maintaining consistency has been fundamental to its success in various markets. Coca-Cola has tailored its packaging and marketing strategies to resonate with local consumers while staying true to its own brand, whether it be a traditional glass bottle in Mexico or sleek cans in Japan.(Slater, 2000, p. 202)

Besides this global dominance, Coca Cola also faces challenges in an increasingly health-conscious world. Fears about sugar intake as well as the rise of healthier substitutes have necessitated innovation and diversification of products by the company. From introducing smaller portion sizes to reformulating its recipes, the multinational beverage corporation is aiming at meeting changing consumer preferences while still capturing the essence of their brands.

Moving forward, Coca-Cola is continuing on exploring new grounds from emerging markets penetration to investments into cutting-edge technologies. Whether it's experimenting with augmented reality experiences or exploring potential CBD-infused beverages, Coca Cola remains committed towards innovative thinking and ahead of trends.

In conclusion, the path of Coca-Cola from a small soda fountain syrup to a world-wide powerhouse is an evidence of its persisting appeal, innovation-oriented approach and cultural communication. Even in its third century, it still symbolizes refreshment, optimism and simple pleasures of life. A bottle of Coca Cola is not merelya drink whether taken privately or with kith or kin but also captures happy moments in a fast moving world.

**Origins and Early Development**

*Dr. Coca-Cola and his efforts behind the evolution of the drink*

John Stith Pemberton, the author of the world-known Coca-Cola, specialized in pharmacy, remedy, and business, and the influence of his output goes again as a way as the gadget itself. On the 8th of July, 1831, John Pemberton was born in Knoxville, Georgia. This unique timeline illustrates the story of someone whose existence is all approximately improvements, perseverance and a regular quest for perfection. The tale of his rise from a humble beginning to his advent of one of the most awarded drinks in human history is a mirrored image of his exemplary creativity and innovation. The invention of carbonated drinks can be traced again to ancient civilizations, where herbal carbonation in springs was enjoyed for its effervescence. However, the first artificially carbonated drink is credited to Joseph Priestley, an English scientist, who determined carbonated water in 1767. Priestley's invention laid the foundation for the improvement of the modern-day tender drink industry. Joseph Priestley's discovery of carbonated water turned into unintended. In 1767, while experimenting with one-of-a-kind glasses, he observed that water infused with carbon dioxide had a pleasing, fizzy flavor. Priestley's work intrigued others, and shortly after, scientists and entrepreneurs started experimenting with carbonation strategies to create a number of flavored drinks. The nineteenth century noticed the rise of soda fountains in Europe and the US. Pharmacists and marketers began adding flavors consisting of fruit syrups to carbonated water, creating a refreshing beverage that gained recognition among customers. These early soda fountains have become social hubs, where humans accrued to experience a fizzy drink and socialize. Coca-Cola, one of the most iconic gentle drinks in records, strains its origins to a pharmacist named John Pemberton. In 1886, Pemberton concocted a caramel-colored syrup in his outdoors in Atlanta, Georgia. He blended this syrup with carbonated water to create a brand new drink, which he first of all advertised as a tonic called "Pemberton's French Wine Coca." Pemberton's tonic contained a combination of coca leaf extract and kola nut, which gave it a completely unique taste and mild stimulating effect. However, as concerns grew over the addictive houses of cocaine, one of the components of the coca leaf, Pemberton replaced it with caffeine-wealthy extracts, ensuring the drink retained its stimulating properties without the controversial aspect. Coca-Cola entered the market as a fountain beverage, served at soda fountains in pharmacies. Its early fulfillment changed largely because of its clean flavor and advertising efforts.
Pemberton's companion and bookkeeper, Frank M. Robinson named the beverage "Coca-Cola" and designed the enduring script brand that stays largely unchanged to this day. (J. Pemberton, 1831-1888; Priestley, 1767; Robinson, n.d.)

*How it became popular as a medicine back in the day*

Coca-Cola's recognition as a medication in its early days may be attributed to several key elements. Firstly, its origins as a medicinal tonic formulated by means of pharmacist John S. Pemberton positioned it within the context of 19th-century health remedies. During this period, various tonics, elixirs, and patent drugs had been marketed as cure-alls for a huge variety of illnesses, from indigestion to nervous issues. Coca-Cola's unique method, which covered coca leaf extract and kola nuts (a herbal supply of caffeine), became marketed as a stimulant and nerve tonic, promising to alleviate fatigue, complications, and even morphine dependence.

The use of coca leaf extract, which incorporates the stimulant cocaine (in a far milder form than pure cocaine), contributed to Coca-Cola's early popularity as a medicinal beverage. In the overdue 19th century,
the psychoactive outcomes of cocaine had been no longer completely understood, and it turned into typically utilized in various tonics and elixirs for its stimulating homes. Coca-Cola's inclusion of this component, together with caffeine-rich kola nuts, possibly contributed to its perceived efficacy as a select-me-up and mood enhancer. Furthermore, Coca-Cola's advertising and distribution techniques played a critical function in its reputation as a medicine. Asa Candler, who acquired the Coca-Cola method in 1888, diagnosed the capacity of the beverage as a business product. Under his management, Coca-Cola became promoted not only as a clean drink but also as a healthy tonic with restorative residences. Advertisements from that generation regularly emphasized Coca-Cola's "invigorating" outcomes and its capacity to combat fatigue and mental fogginess.

Overall, Coca-Cola's popularity as a remedy in its early life may be attributed to a combination of factors, which includes its formulation as a stimulant tonic, powerful advertising and marketing strategies, considerable distribution, and association with healthy advantages throughout a generation when such treatments had been especially famous.

*How did Dr. Pemberton sell it to Asa Candler*

In 1888 AS Candler, a widely known businessman and innovator who owned Candlerer Industries, sold the rights to Coca-Cola from Pemberton for $2300. Pemberton may additionally have lacked the assets, expertise, or infrastructure needed to scale up production and efficiently market Coca-Cola on a bigger scale. Asa Candler, together with his enterprise acumen and mounted industrial infrastructure, should offer the assets and abilities essential to increase Coca-Cola's attainment and maximize its capacity.

Pemberton would possibly have had self belief in Asa Candler's imaginative and prescient for Coca-Cola and believed that Candler should increase the beverage to greater heights than Pemberton ought to achieve independently. Candler's song report as a hit businessman and innovator may additionally have reassured Pemberton that Coca-Cola might be in successful fingers.(Candler Industries, 1888)

During Candler's live performance, the Coca-Cola Company unrolled a grand advertising and advertising and marketing blitz to intensify the merchandising of the drink and develop the logo iconography.

Chandler coupled numerous upcoming improvements and methodologies to reach this goal with such ideas like advertisements, merchandising, and distribution that could substantially rework the beverage area and make Coca-Cola the arena chief.

*What did Candler do to the brand?*

Given that Candler took the reins of what is nowadays known as Coca-Cola's most mounted product, putting in a brand that became identifiable and unique, with the intention to separate this product from its competitors became one of the first matters he did. This became to in addition his purpose with the aid of spending an awful lot on advertising, advertising and exposure that accentuated the particular flavor, taste, and refreshment of the product's packaging. The media outreach bulls-eye of Candler protected revealed media including newspapers and magazines tallying up with signage and billboards that allows you to seize a national as well as an international customers. Candler similarly superior the first-in-the-magnificence tactics of using merchandising techniques of couponing, sampling, and product placement. He began handing out loose samples at public places consisting of fairs and events; the ones attracted others and supplied the base for similar business sports.

In addition to this, in step with Candler, coupons had been introduced which could be redeemed at soda fountains for an unfastened Coca-Cola glass if clients bought it there. So, there has been an immediate response to profits from the very start. Candler made this real for the Coca-Cola Company, given that it flew without delay to enlargement and increase power by using aggressive advertising and marketing and fruitful partnerships. He did this by building a manufacturing plant where gaseous plants have been bottled and deployed in shops across America, which made the Coca-Cola emblem reach greater even in the far off regions. He additionally effectively hooked up a prestigious network of bottlers and distributors, presenting them with the rights to produce and promote Coca-Cola in unique territories. Candler's growth paintings marched first into the other country, in 1906 Coca-Cola debuted making in which its venture is set in Canada. This marked the primary recognition in worldwide enlargement, as the beverage succeeded in thriving inside the marketplace worldwide at a panoramic pace. By the beginning of the 20 th Century Coca-Cola became acquainted and celebrated all through exceptional cultures, in both continents because of its recognizable brand and the famous contour bottle as a symbol of refreshing and amusement.

*Early Marketing Strategies*

The methods of advertising and marketing and strategies of Coca- Cola were the best tools that made it possible for the company to dominate the industry at international level. Through their impactful televised advertisements, and later clever marketing strategies, Coca-Cola has been unrelenting in their constant evolution to remain competitive and current. During the "Share a Coke" campaign, which was launched in 2011, Coca-Cola bottles came in personalized versions, with printed names all over, which helped in forging a likable social media trending content and customer interaction. On top of that, Coca-Cola has used its sponsorship of significant sports events such as the FIFA World Cup and the Olympic Games, to penetrate the grassroots market and increase its brand awareness on the local level as well. (Van Mesdag, 2000, p.75).

Advertising has been a prominent promise of gain to a street vendor advertising her flower-seller's shop. She advertises to shape people's spending and affect people's thoughts of what is popular. To Coca-Cola, advertising is number one to that brand method because of the primary nature of inception, allowing it to do the job of establishing a strong emotional association with customers and trigger their audience picture of joy, happiness, and unity even more powerful.

The Early Years: "Drink Coca-Cola"

First decades of the 20th century were marked by Coca Cola's dispersion efforts aimed at pushing the brand into a new level with a consumption of the beverage as drink of choice for all occasions. Coca-Cola spread across using print ads, signage, and promotional articles to be a drink that takes folk together and makes their recreational moments special. The words "Drink Coca-Cola" which accompany the logo have become as common as the logo itself, appearing on billboards, public soda fountains, and sometimes even the sides of houses. This turns Coca-Cola into an inseparable part from the American tradition.


The Birth of Santa Claus: Coca-Cola's Christmas Campaigns

One of the longest living things in Coca Cola is linking up the new image of Santa Claus to the throwaway culture. In 1931, Coca-Cola gave the assignment of creating the works of art that shows Santa Claus to the artist Haddon Sundblom for use in their Christmas advertising and marketing endeavor. If his image is to remain contemporary, then other artists will try to do better with his jolly and rosy-cheeked Santa. (Krishna, 2005)
He will pop up once in a while on printed ads, billboards and video commercials and show the same old face. Coca-cola's Christmas campaigns, by the same token, not only enhanced brand image but also, in fact, helped to form if not by then modern mythology about Santa Claus.

"It's the Real Thing": Coca-Cola's Evolution within the Sixties and Seventies

The late Sixties and early Seventies (1960s and 1970s) witnessed the presence of considerable cultural and social change, reflected in the Coca-Cola advertising. The new slogan was introduced "It's the Real Thing," this changed the way Coke advertised, refocusing the viewer to authenticity and purity with Coca-Cola as the only thing that had not changed with the world. Thus, it correlated to the present day, making the company timeless in the process. Then, opposite to this, ads from that time singled out freedom, compatibility, and the timelessly celebrated enchantment of the Coca-Cola, which impressed audiences all around the world.(Sivny, 2007)

"Mean Joe Greene" and Other Memorable Commercials

In the 60s advertisements of the Coca Cola Company used the technique of storytelling. This is how they created their jocular and memorable classified ads, which left a lasting effect on lifestyles of people all over the world.  Such a mechanic as the NFL "Mean Joe taught us words of wisdom. "It was during a momentary time break that Hovik entered the world of passionate supporters of Coke-Cola, and he became a star on the run, receiving several internationally awarded prizes for his humorous writing and many imitations on TV and media.  The success of Hovik was noticed by other secret advertisers, including "I'd buy the world a Coke" and "Hilltop" ads.

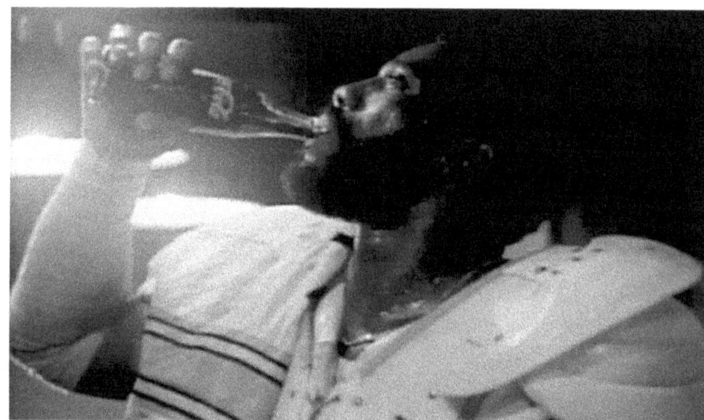

The digital age: Coca-Cola on the internet

Nowadays, Coke envisions that it has to proceed with product innovations and build its advertising techniques to adjust to this digital era. The new media and the interaction is the special way Coca-Cola is close with the consumers and provides them with an exciting journey crossing boundaries of geography and then be bonded together. from guerrilla marketing to customers co-creation, Coca-Cola has exploited the chance of digitality high as a further vehicle for their brand message and have connected to new audiences.

In the end, Coca-Cola and its advertising campaigns became a trendsetter from the early marketing strategies to promote the brand as a clean drink for changing or developing the way we do things, to the latest campaigns where various cultures, ideas and trends are celebrated around the planet, it has gone a long way symbolizing team spirit, happiness and diversity. The cola company has always used its ads as the way of establishing an intimate relationship between the brand and consumers. Coca-Cola stays loyal to their client tastes as well as possibilities and adapts its image through advertising campaigns. This will surely remain the key characteristic of the Coca-Cola brand.

**Expansion of Coca-Cola across the United States in the late 19th and early 20th Centuries**

Impact on Culture

Cultural impact of the Coca-Cola brand goes by its composition of drinks and beyond. It is interwoven into the fibers of popular subculture, shaping cultural styles, rituals, and social modes of living across the planet. The marketing and promotion of the soft drink brand Coca-Cola centered on the use of sharp slogans, popular jingles, and memorable imagery appeared universally, leading to the phenomenon of populism manifested as cultural icons such as Santa Claus belonging to the brand were introduced earlier in the 20th century. This addition has strengthened the current conceptions of Christmas similarly to those taken from folklore. Coca- Cola has borrowed and celebrated American culture from a long time back by placing their company's logos and symbols inside their products like stuffed- to- cups and posters that have had the shape of coke bottles, from the classic contour bottles to the timeless red and white logo. The image is now a cliche of how one looks at American culture, emphasizing on shared values such as liberty, democracy and hope. (Ocansey and Enahoro, 2014)

Coca Cola, as a symbol of American culture influences people's minds through the brand designs that demonstrate the cultural bond of Americans and their customs. The Coca-Cola product line also includes ice-cooled beverages, coffee, tea, and sparkling water. A range of these products is found exclusively in the U. S. , such as the classic Coke flavor, Diet Coke for instance, and the popular Fanta orange soda. Additionally, these products are heavily exported to numerous countries, making the Coca-Cola name widely recognizable worldwide. (TCCC report, 2020)

The ethnic diversity, as a broad variant, comprises such parts as speech, traditions, customs, beliefs and lifestyles. Taking into account the poignancy of acknowledging and embracing cultural differences, the Coca-Cola brand has done everything possible to include the components reflecting the cultural heritage in its advertisement campaigns, while on the other hand keeping its famous logo and values.

Coca-Cola is aware of the fact that expositions and traditions bridge people together as they are the umbilical cord of cultural identity and make a community spirit to rise up. Coca-Cola provides space for diverse cultures, by that, it often inlays celebratory issues and symbols into ad campaigns. This led to the symbolization of comfort, traditions and celebrations with the Coca-Cola brand. Whichever cultural celebration, be it the Lunar New Year in Asia, Diwali in India, or Christmas in western world, Coca-Cola always makes use of this occasion to connect with the very emotional part of a human and to put a shame about feelings such as happiness, togetherness, and nostalgia.

Speaking of global marketing and the brand's efforts to adapt to foreign culture, "Coca-Cola" applies its own advertising plans and techniques to different societies. The company also uses its advertising campaigns and its organization activities to promote diversity and inclusion. By extending messages related to harmony, popularity and equality to all, regardless of their social status, Coca Cola makes one feel part of a big-recognised familyCoca-Cola, which promotes diversity by highlighting styles and colors also through advertising and storytelling, thereby underlining its willingness to celebrate the diversity of global cultures.(Bennett & Blythe, 2002, p.6).

Coca-Cola is often seen working with cultural institutions, recreation centers, sports events and other influencers who are connected to various crowds of people, enabling Coca-Cola to communicate its brand values in different spheres. During collaboration with music fairs, film festivals, and the celebrity endorsements the brand shows itself as a brand deeply rooted in different cultural aspects and being a part of popular culture and remains culturally relevant.

*Expansion and Growth*

Marketing Strategies

While brand building began with the introduction of the distinctive bottles, eventually they became the center of the general advertising and corporate promotions run by Candler. Candler put in too much selling and advertising and therefore tried transferring his strategy to the general US people. A schedule for ad campaigns centering around the iconic tone, flavor, and rejuvenating quality was the first that the entrepreneur of Coca-Cola thought up to establish a strong visual image for the brand. (Kant et al., 2008, p.40)

In addition, he refined the advanced actors of promotion employed by sample, couponing, and product placement. He was offering handouts to people who happened to pass by in public places like festivals and special events; these samplers did not only attract more guests but also served as foundation upon which a business venture could be developed.(Weisert, D., 2001) Furthermore, according to Candler the soda bottle cap also doubled up as a coupon that when carried to a soda fountain, could be redeemed for a free Coca-Cola glass upon purchase. But in contrast, it could be said the household did not have incomes at all and hence there was no response to any income from the start.

Leading the way, aside from conventional marketing approach, Coca-Cola implemented an ingenious advertising campaign involving, but not limited to, couponing and sampling of its product. He spelled the nation's name with his products by giving Coca-Cola samples during his presentations across the country. Then his clients really wanted Coca-Cola drinks to quench their thirst. And it has become a part of the positive reviews that have been spreading among customers, raising the same. Moreover, he increased the cost of Coca-Cola and targeted specific soda fountains by giving discounts in the form of free glasses of Coca-Cola. In this way, he achieved two marketing emphases – price reduction and sales increase. Coca-cola deployed marketing and advertising approaches which eventually facilitated its "worldwide dominance. "The company has never ceased in its exploration of fresh reveals regarding promoting and marketing. Strategic partnerships were also done on logos with the principal aim of being relevant in the changing market environment. The social media phenomena titled "Share a Coke" produced and launched by Coca-Cola in 2011 placed individual names on Coke canisters, unleashing a social media storm and rekindling brand relationships. Moreover, Coca-Cola's sponsorship of highly popular sports events such as FIFA World Cup and Olympics helped the brand to spread around all over the country.

By deploying some strategic entry FDI techniques, the company not only developed a firm position abroad but also became a local brand in a foreign country. One of the key things we did in our early days include branding into local depots such as supermarkets and bottling shops where managers were well known with area markets and distribution networks. (Daniels, 2011, p.775) These exclusive permits allow the licensers to exercise control over the production and distribution of the Coca-Cola brand name in the given regions. As a result, the company can expand its operations fast so that it can enter new markets easily.

In rural places, the market achievement of Coke was even more driven by the company's promotional and branding activities where the company managed to plant the passion of familiarity and belonging in consumers' hearts and minds for the company worldwide. By clearing the great campaigns of advertising and marketing, sponsoring sports occasions that are important, and creating during the nodes of the towns the extent to reach the local customers, Coca-Cola has become the icon of happiness, fun and alsothe community all through different cultures and languages.

One of major strategies in the strategies of Coca-Cola to reduce the cultural range is the national and the localized advertising campaigns. Instead of borrowing the adapted method and producing it on all platforms, Coca-Cola tends to work closely with the local advertising bodies, cultural specialists, and influencers to create campaigns that favor what is relevant in every country. The brand does that through integration of local languages, imagery, music and language-specific elements which make the campaigns relevant and extremely effective in diverse markets. Amongst the major things that Coca-Cola employs to ensure its messages are passed across different cultures is the integration of sponsorships and neighborhood partnerships. The strategy utilized by Coca-Cola Company for cultural visibility involves tapping into occasions and events in the South, working with such organizations, and aligning its brand with those of respected cultural influencers, among others. Coca-Cola decides how best it can give back to its community. As the example one, Coca-Cola supports its nearby sports team, band, or any cultural occasion. (Carroll, 1991)


1. Branding Strategy

- Leveraging Iconic Brand Equity: The iconic presence of the company, its symbol equalization and the brand popularity worldwide, give the chance to the business's diverse line of products. The Coca-Cola company uses its logo name in such a way that customers start believing, they know this drink and they trust the product. Another reason is that Coca-Cola's logo is commonly used to increase the level of sales and market share in different beverage classes.
- Brand Extension and Sub-Branding: Coca-Cola uses brand extension strategy to place new accessories that are known brands, including Minute Maid for juices and Dasani for the bottled water. Sub-branding will let Coca-cola use their powerful original logo and at the same time differentiate your products inside particular fields and consumers.
- Brand Positioning and Messaging: All the products within Coca-Cola portfolio are also positioned and fortified to offer its clients a variety of special purposes throughout the day or in other activity preferences. The organization utilizes such pronouncements as pleasure, flavor, convenience, and the pampering of lifestyle traits as it is coherent with the client's opt for as well as the environment characteristics.


2. Marketing Strategy

- Customer-centric innovation: The advertisement strategies of Coca-Cola arise from innovative consumer-centered approaches that are supported with consumers' in-depth insights into emerging consumer preferences and market trends. The employer will source for research, development and invention of new merchandise, flavors and packaging that fulfill the customers target and differentiate Coca-Cola from competitors.
- Multichannel Marketing: Coca-Cola performs multi-channel advertising to communicate with the consumers by means of several touch points with traditional marketing, digital media channels, experiential marketing, shops and shops. It operates with both direct selling tactics and network marketing to grow awareness, increase engagement and eventually boost sales among different populations and market segments.

- Integrated Management Campaign: Coca- Cola is a multi-channel inclusive campaign aimed at communicating a brand message and a story that is sometimes juicy. This way of marketing these brands apply story-telling, emotional magic, and cultural significance to connect with consumers on a deeper level, boost brand interaction and loyalty.

*Bottling and Distribution*

The iconic Coca-Cola bottle design and its Significance

The unquestionable Coca-Cola bottle mold is obsolete in all continents of the globe as a sign of the beverage itself, but people also now start to connect it with the future, past, and generation of the Coca-Cola brand. In this detailed endeavor, we can delve into the historical, cultural and universal impact of Coca-Cola bottle design, which started as a simple box and has evolved into a corporate defining icon with a worldwide reputation. This design being a product of the useful services of the Root Glass Company of Terre Haute, Indiana, is a design that is typically referred to as the "contour bottle" or the "hobble-skirt bottle" owing to its curves that are beautifying, and its flute base. Provided only with the resource of the pod from which the cocoa is made, the irregular styled bottle appeared unlike any beverage container of its time but, with its curvy silhouette, it was identified also if it was smashed into thirds.

Contoured bottles with replacement caps were patented in 1915 shortly thereafter only Coca-Cola brand recognized. The distinctive bottle has solidified as the brand image that's emblematic of the logo's identification and core values. The contour bottle, which got patent in 1915 and became popular with "Coca-Cola" introduced in 1915, became a sort of a visual trademark of the personality and values of this Brunad, recognizable all over the world. The shape bottle was produced with such pronounced contour and also referred to as the "hobble skirt" bottle, as it was unlike any other beverage bottle in the market at that time. The Root Glass Company designed this bottle; its unique and attractive shape helped the bottle to be quickly distinguished easily and remembered. The iconic Coca-Cola bottle and its distinctive design gave it a significant edge over the competitors and it was now solely connected with the brand. The curvaceous contour of this Coke bottle was also there as constant reminding so that the public could keep remembering and recognize the brand. This unique contour became a visual shorthand, faithfully representing not only the brand's famous flavor and the numerous visual links associated with it, but also the distinct memories and feelings it elicits. In this way Coca-Cola was able to strengthen its brand identity by means of which it extracted itself from the crowd of competitor's drinks.

The outline and shape of the bottle allowed the sellers and consumers to add the sense of memories and tradition which make a strong connection between the both of them emotionally. The brand's timeless visual has been the emblem of a simple lifestyle and dispelled the similarity of the shared ones whereas Coca-Cola belongs to your past and future. It is this emotional association which drew customers closer to the brand and created the kind of long-term commitment that no commercial approach could ever rival. The success of the contour bottle can be credited due to its conscientious package design and its market creation (logo-constructing) feature. In contrast to standard straight-bodied bottles, our team thought that contour shape would be of inspiration, creating not only cozy products but also making it easy to grasp and bring with. Moreover, a visual identity and logo additionally appeared because window dressings differentiate it from competitors allowing Coca-Cola to stand out on store shelves and in ads.
The rising up of Coca-Cola is clearly visible through its smart marketing tactics and strategic placement that have dwarfs it into a cultural icon loved all over the world which is more than just a useful box as it represents American optimism, innovation, and not to mention, cleverness.

From its days as an American Cola brand to its later years as a global symbol of the product, the contour bottle has always given a form to its identity. From the busy streets of New York City to the villages in the African and Asian continents, the bottle silhouette of Coca-Cola instantly became recognizable which not only evoked feelings of nostalgia, familiarity, and a sense of shared humanity but, most importantly, that became the embodiment of something that is truly, genuinely and deeply unique. The marketing and advertising campaigns of Coca-Cola made use of the contour bottle's electricity, piercing in the depths of the human psyche, to ignite a spark, connect people emotionally, and deliver common themes like pride, joy, and attachment. (Lee & Maxfield, 2015)

Up till now, therefore, the Coca-Cola container has built up some significant adjustments and adaptations to address the evolution of the client choices and produce technologies. But the basic contour line style of the bottle has held true in most of them; the manufacturer has also designed the 'diet' and 'mini' versions to satisfy different consumer segments and occasions. Furthermore, the manufacture of the latest materials like plastic and aluminum has enabled Coca-Cola to devise alternative yet similar structures and famous logos which are evident in their original contour bottle.


Finally, the Coca-Cola bottle design becomes a lovable icon of brand's intelligence, creativity and cultural icon. Over the years, starting with the word of mouth from the fight against the counterfeiting and until the time as the universally recognized icon enjoyed by all people of different ages and social backgrounds, the contour bottle represents the values, history, intelligence and creativity of making the CocaCola trademark. As the dynamically changing Coca-Cola keeps on adapting to the fashion and the market, the distinctive form of the Coca-Cola bottle is never forgotten. That is the proof of the magical power of designto sculpt our minds and shape not only our thoughts but our personalities and collective identity.

Coca-Cola
In the Distinctive Bottle
est.1886

1899
1900
1916
1957

1899
1900
1915
1916
1957
1986

*Coca-Cola's Advertising Campaigns and their Impact on Popular Culture*

The introduction of Santa Claus as a trademark by Coca-Cola

Advertisement and Shaping Subculture by Coked-Cola became the most successful and popular in the world. From widely recognizable taglines to memorable classified ads, Coca-Cola marketing has always been used as a strategy to get attached to consumers, to this sensation, and to be remembered. The exploration is centered upon Coca-Cola and its ad campaigns that shaped 20th century to digital age lifestyles.

Advertisement makes use of the power of the creative imagination to mold the patron behavior and models lifestyle. This marketing strategy has been key to Coca-Cola with the corporation branding practicewhich is rich in history starting from the inception of the firm; it has an established emotional connection with customers and hence the strong brand image of happiness, joy and togetherness.

In the beginning of the 20th century, Coca-Cola's advertising stressed mainly on the idea of consuming the beverage as a quick and revitalizing drink for both fun and daily moments of life. Coca-Cola appeared in print ads of various kinds, signboards, and giveaway materials and it usurped this position of communal drink which would lift peoples' spirits up and beautify their moments of shared serenity. The "Drink Coca-Cola" slogan has become interchangeable with the logo, including on billboards, soda fountains, even the sides of someday, Coke is enrooted to American history.

Presenting the new image of Santa Claus is one of the leading Leipzig-verbindend elements established by Coca- Cola. In the year 1931, Coca-Cola commissioned artist Haddon Sundblom to develop these illustrations used in its commercial advertising and marketing campaigns of Santa Claus for Christmas.
Sundblom's jolly, rosy-cheeked Santa has been replaced with the new one which is the no less famous character depiction of the classic Santa Claus, the figure appearing in print adverts, billboards and television commercials for decades being called back. If it was not for Coca-Cola's Christmas campaigns the picture of the modern Santa Claus would not have been developed through the brand's activities in this period.

Coca-Cola did cultural exchange and social change in the 60's and 70's dramatically which was manifested in the beverage company's commercial. The advent of the "It's The Real Thing" credo symbolized a change in direction towards the real thing and purity gets people convinced to buy more classic Coca-Cola products that react to a growing custom worldwide. These commercials stressed upon variety in their approach, cohesion and the 'time-proven magic' of Coca-Cola that they were looking to build connections in a brand way across the globe.

During the second part of the 20th century, Coca-Cola advertised a bunch of ads that brought about a modification of the American lifestyle System. For instance, the same approach is used on ads to market opposing teams such as the Griffin, who slash their opponents in an on the field battle akin to the "Mean Joe." Instead, Green, who is depicted as a Coca-Cola fan, graduated to instant fame, flooding the media with tons of praises and parodies to the point of creating a wave of such phenomenon in the pop culture piece that later on produced other famous hidden ads like " I'd like to buy the World a Coke" and "Hilltop," that not so insistently, but powerfully alluded.

In the twenty-first century, Coca-Cola has continued to innovate and increase its marketing strategies to satisfy the demands of the virtual world. Through social media initiatives, on-line video streaming and interactive campaigns, Coca-Cola is connecting with customers in new and creative ways, developing interactive studies and connections with a global marketplace constructed on its' . Visually inside the From competitive advertising and marketing campaigns to client-designed merchandise Coca -Cola has embraced the digital age as a manner to enlarge its brand message and reach new audiences

Ultimately, Coca-Cola's advertising and advertising campaigns have left an indelible mark on popular subcultures, starting with early tries to put itself as a smooth beverage for behavior-changing activities , all thoughts and developments around the sector to contemporary campaigns celebrating range, group spirit and happiness . Cola has constantly used marketing as a manner to connect with clients on a deep emotional stage While Coca-Cola continues and adapts to changing customer tastes and opportunities , itsadvertising and advertising campaigns will undoubtedly remain the cornerstone of its iconic identification.

**The introduction of Santa Claus as a trademark by Coca-Cola**

The emergence of Santa Claus as an advertising and marketing and advertising image through Coca-Cola is a captivating tale along side rich statistics of any enduring beverage symbol and loved person of Santa Claus -
We will explore the have an effect on this commercial has had at the long term and advertising marketing campaign on way of life and customer behavior. Synonymous with Christmas cheer and now philanthropy, Santa Claus has an extended and sundry report based on mythology, folklore, and cultural impacts across the vicinity. Although pictures of nowadays Santa Claus are often related to yellow playing cards it lasts approximately although white beard and pink cheeks originate in ancient myths and legends can be restored and analyzed. The

origins of Santa Claus may be traced back to the 4th-century Christian bishop Saint Nicholas, recognized for his generosity and compassion towards the terrible and needy. Over the centuries, the legend of Saint Nicholas developed and merged with diverse folk traditions, along with the Dutch determination of Sinterklaas and the English man or woman of Father Christmas, to create the present day photograph of Santa Claus. The modern-day-day portrayal of Santa Claus acquired a full-size beautification in 1823 with the e-book of *A Visit from St. Nicholas* furthermore referred to as *The Night Before Christmas.* Written via Clement Clarke Moore, this desired poem depicted Santa Claus as a jolly vintage man who travels via way of sleigh and provides objects to children on Christmas Eve, cementing maximum of the acquainted tropes associated with the individual.

In the nineteenth century, the American illustrator Thomas Nast accomplished a pivotal function in shaping the seen identity of Santa Claus. Through a series of illustrations posted in Harper's Weekly, Nast depicted Santa Claus as a portly parent with a white beard, crimson in shape, and sack of toys, organizing a number of the visible motifs that might come to outline the individual for generations to return. Although many papers depicted SantaClaus at some point inside the 19th and early twentieth centuries, it turned into Coca-Cola that solidified his iconic image in a century of iconic advertising campaigns of this 20th problem. Coca-Cola commissioned Hayden Sundblom, an accomplished business artist, to carry Santa Claus into their lives in advertising campaigns.
Drawing inspiration from Moore's poetry and Nast's illustrations, Sundblom created a heat, friendly and approachable Santa Claus who embodies the spirit of Christmas and the joy of sharing Coca-Cola with cherished ones. Sundblom's iconic portrait of Santa Claus for Coca-Cola was first regarded in 1931, displaying a wide white beard, sparkling eyes, a brilliant crimson fork adorned with white leather-based and perception appealing circle. These snapshots, counted in print advertisements, billboards and promotional substances. They have quickly ended up being synonymous with the holiday season. This feature helped solidify Coca-Cola's .

The introduction of Santa Claus as an advertising and marketing symbol by means of Coca-Cola is a testament to the energy of marketing to form cultural discourses and have an impact on purchaser conduct. Through images of Santa Claus' image, Coca-Cola helped give a boost to current images of desirable tourism too. As we bask inside the magic of Christmas every twelve months, Coca-Cola Santa is a reminder of the pleasure, warmth and harmony that outline the vacation season for hundreds and heaps of human beings across the location.

## Global Expansion and International Marketing

Coca-Cola's journey to global recognition resembles a captivating tale. Originating as a modest beverage in Atlanta, Georgia, it has evolved into a universally acknowledged symbol. This narrative will uncover the pivotal triumphs and strategic decisions that have propelled Coca-Cola's global expedition. The story commenced in the early 20th century when Coca-Cola made its debut in the United States. Venturing far from its roots, the company had already achieved success by establishing a bottling facility in Canada back in 1906. Progressing into Cuba, Panama, and Puerto Rico swiftly ensued after these initial endeavors laid the groundwork for an expanded international presence and set the stage for further development.

World War II was the main catalyst for the lightning fast dispersal of Coca-Cola around the globe. While the company was fighting in the war, Coca-Cola decided to give the American troops anticipated free drinks in the far-away units. The policy not only helped their troops' morale but also, Coca-Cola entered the new markets at the warfront. Towards the end of the fight, Coca Cola had already established itself in 60 international locations and territories, so it became reasonably easy for the company to start an international expansion against print.

The follow-up after the war, Coca-Cola took various measures of economic recovery in Europe and Asia in addition to a larger overseas network. One of the various challenges is the well-established tap water system for the manufacturers of bottled water in France, Italy, and other countries.

Thanks to the fact that Coca-Cola is the official sponsor of the Olympic Games, the company has had an enormous impact on the level of world-wide visibility of its brand and its relationship to the world of sports and adolescent lifestyle. From the 1928 Amsterdam Olympics onwards, Coca-Cola regularly cooperated with the Olympic Movement and supported sporting events and athletes from various Olympic Games. After a century, Coca-Cola still has solid partners overseas and at home which are responsible forproviding international boost to the brand ideas of optimism, friendship, and enthusiasm.

Being a part of Coca-Cola's plan for international development, Coca-Cola's strategy includes the aim to achieve more popularity in countries with quickly growing populations like Latin America, Asia, and Africa. To account for the big boom the company is ending up in emerging markets, Coca-Cola established the manufacturing units, sales networks and the appropriate advertisement and branding campaigns that fits into every market perfectly. With such a regionalization method, Coca-Cola has immensely grown its market-shares and brand awareness, which has consequently seen it being regarded as a dependent and beloved brand in different geographical areas of the environment.

Coca-Cola Company in recent years has been known as the one movement among online trade transformation and e-trading projects to enhance firmwide operations in the global market. This business has utilized digital technologies, data analytics and online systems to bring customers closer to community, deeply personalized marketing messages, and well-organized distribution channels. Coca-Cola has done it by getting on a bus of e-change trends and accepting the changing way customers behave. This positioning of their brand gained them victory in the virtual world.

On a summary note, Coca-Cola's breakthrough in the international market has truly been the result of its doggedness, magnificent strategic vision, and the customer-centricity business philosophy. The journey of Coca-Cola from its hometown starting point in Atlanta to the global competitiveness stardom status has to be worth narrating. The company conquered many challenges, made endless opportunities and left its mark on the world stage. With its legacy in place, enduring values, and a highly energized as well as successfully focused 'Always Coke' approach that has made Coca-Cola a super-brand across the globe, this iconic brand continues to inspire and refresh its clients even after centuries, assuring its place in people's hearts for a very, very long time to come.(Van Heerden & Barter, 2008).

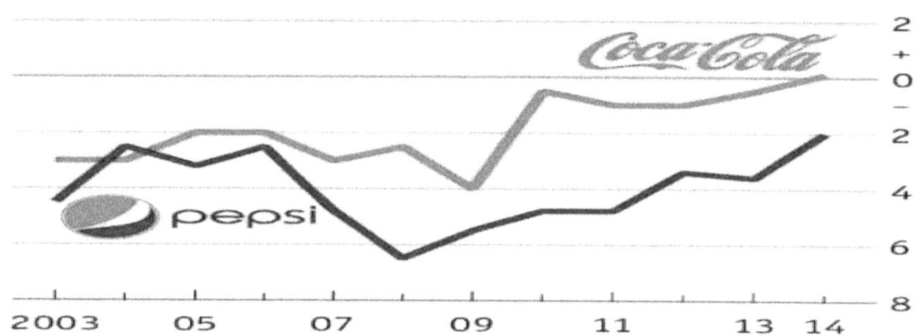

## Product Diversification and Brand Extensions

The amazing arrival of Diet Coke in 1982 was a remarkable moment in Coca-Cola's history, which proved to be a battlefield where Coke stepped into the growing market of lower calorie products. Coke became very popular excluding fitness-aware people with its consumption and broadened Coca-Cola's product variety beyond the famous cola brand. Through this differentiation Coca Cola managed to cover new market segments and serve the consumers' contrary choice behavior. (Walsh, 2003)

In 1960, Coca-Cola company had acquired Minute Maid Corporation, the leader producer of fruit drinks and juices, and to some extent it has entered the soft beverages market. The brand's strategic acquisition multiplied the prospect of a diversified product assortment and the chance of exploiting a maturing need of wellness beverages. From the outset, the Coca-Cola Company has expanded its field of activities not only in the carbonated beverage market, but also in the international non-carbonated beverages arena through acquisitions, collaborations, and spin-offs to make Coca-Cola and the industry a dominant force globally.

In 1982 Diet Coke was introduced to the public which was seen as the cutting-edge innovation as it addressed the critical gap of low-calorie beverage which was a major missing component of Coca-Cola. Chasing the approach of "no sugar" together with pure, awesome taste, Diet Coke became a number one choice for health-conscious customers wanting to minimize calorific value they take in without any sacrifice in taste factors. As you know, we become the chief commercial operations pioneer of the quickly developing market for the targeting-based planning and light refreshments segment.

Diet Coke gave birth to the Coca-Cola Zero in 2005 that sought to follow suit the ladder of almost sugarless beverages collecting more prospective customers from the segment of 0-calorie market. Coca-Cola Zero has joined the diet drink niche market with Diet Coke but focuses on the younger generation and presents fundamental resemblance in taste to original Coca-Cola. It tapped into the strength of its name image fairness and exploration talent to see the stairway of success start as quickly as the product was being released in the marketplace, thus adding to the diet drinks share of Coca-Cola Company.

Coca-Cola discontinued Coca-Cola Life in 2013 in order to answer consumers' demand for natural sweeteners and low-calorie alternatives. The brew of cane sugar with stevia leaf extract was the combination used in Coca-Cola Life, and this introduced consumers to a Coke version with fewer calories and a natural touch to sweeten it up. Coke Life, whose tagline was "Taste the new tradition," spoke to health-conscious clients who love the spicy taste, but also wanted to have a share of their calories and be part of the Coca-cola line.

Coca-Cola Freestyle which was officially introduced in 2009, is the true embodiment of Coke's innovation as it afforded customers with the ability to "freestyle " and make their own sort of drinks through its revolutionary self-serve dispensers. In the end, Coca-Cola Freestyle had more than one hundred unique flavors and blends offered to buyers who asked to customize their beverage enjoyment and try accuracy among varieties. The Coca-Cola Freestyle is in actuality, not only a remarkable platform to engage customers and enthusiast them, but also an intelligent platform where Coca-Cola can gather much more extensive data insights into purchasing decisions and buyer behavior.

As the market requested liquid and cognitive drinks in a short time, Coca-Cola released the Coca-Cola energy beverage in 2019. The new Coca-Cola Energy, with the well-known flavor of Coke combined with caffeine and various nutrients, is a clean and energizing beverage choice that helps initiate the active lifestyles of customers. Coca-Cola managed to broaden the product range and now it is beyond the scope of traditional colas, providing even more spaces for the audience to choose the beverage and grow inside the dynamic and fast-expanding health drink niche.

Moreover, with the advent of new Coca-Cola products like Diet Coke, Coca-Cola Zero and so on, and the company's constant agenda to have innovation, creativity and being customer-centric there is no doubt that Coca-Cola will continue to be forward-looking and strategically dynamic. Through innovative flexibility to meet and overtake customer alternatives and expansive market trends, Coca-Cola increasingly expanded its brand image and successfully opened new market segments, thus proving to be a leading beverage company worldwide. However, the company will continue to innovate and expand its offers applying its iconic brand name and insight of consumer needs for more employment and making additional value for all stakeholders in the world.

**One such product that diversifies in the well grown market is that of Zero Coke.**

In the arena of carbonate soft drinks Zero Coke can be seen to be a fresh and new drink which has endeared it to the worldwide public and is a symbol of a new trend. As health and well-being consciousness prevail as the most popular movements around the world, one of the alternatives is Zero Coke to people who are interested in taking on the right balance between healthiness and refreshment.

Primordially, the main characteristics of Zero Coke are low sugar, low calories, and similar beverage grounds with the conventional carbonated soda. Due to this combination of solutions, consumers can now be assured that uncontrolled sugar consumption will not result in diabetes and obesity. The drink one enjoys as a guilt-free treat gives one a feeling of pure delight as it has the vibrant flavor of the traditional cola and allows the customers to achieve their health goals.

The success story of Zero Coke suggests consumers' longing for radically changed preferences as much as its implications for the environment and nutrition. The brand has their users in mind when it comes to environment conservation, besides packaging which is green in color and buying objects responsibly, the environmental impact has been highly reduced. This will be in accordance with the view of consumers who are key to environmentally friendly production and they try to opt for the ones which benefit nature.

Note should be Zero Coke is what the soft drink industry believes in and develop it as a significant factor which wellness is the primary reason why it is. The fusion of the caloric content for the casual Coke aficionado and the health benefits for the fitness enthusiast makes it a choice across social and generational lines.

Furthermore, Zero Coke completely changed the meaning of the brand, despite being a product, into a synonym sense that defines an individual's way of life beyond that of a typical soda. It is one of examples when ideal life becomes real, when someone can fully enjoy the marvelous small moments not ruining one's health. It is the generation that gives much significance to healthy, tasty, and sustainability, which bears resemblance to the brand's endorsement.

***Product's USP***

Coca-Cola Zero is a tremendous intruder that makes us happy. We should not consider anything to lead guilt-unfastened lives, having some people handy new beverages to decide on. Rather than the prerequisites to maximum of these active customers, Coca-Cola Zero has become a beacon for people striving to experience the delight of the classic cola without jeopardizing their health and fitness goals, through its well developed USP that is depended upon its 0 calorie content.

Caloric Liberation:

Coca-Cola Zero's big achievement in that its Calor Simple is now a zero calorie composition is its number one publicity strategy. The soda market has displayed a rapid transition as beverage makers target products as healthy diets become increasingly popular among health conscious customers. Coca-Cola Zero captures this high-growth trend and consistently offers a cola flavor that neither breaks away from this tradition nor is contrary to the zero calorie project.

A most interesting solution is the zero-calorie method for customers that want to manage their calorie intake without compromising the taste. Because of this feature, "Coke Quizero" as it is known to popular clients, is a perfect option for the people on diets that limit calories, weight watchers, and people with clinical conditions that require them to alter their consumption of sugar and energy.

Indulgence without Compromise: The Taste Contradiction

The sense of taste is our very first sense that notifies us about meals. One might think that zero-calorie might always taste less delicious but this brand uses the expertise and comes up with innovative sugar substitutes that compete with the very best. For those who would love to sip on a traditional Coca-Cola flavor while losing out on the extra calories, the flavor profile created by the Coca-Cola specialists gives a worldly cola drink feeling.

The USP (unique selling point) of Coca-Cola Zero is this paradoxical gold flavor intended to attract consumers. A wide category of customers with a healthier lifestyle who can also reduce the number of cravings is the key aim of our brand. Coca-Cola Zero is an intelligent drink that pursues two, at first sight, different objectives: a high level of enjoyment along with health and well-being.

Innovative Sweetening Technology

Innovative sweetening era is the crucial trading point of Coca-Cola Zero's captivating a zero-calorie range. A two-sweetener blend – acesulfame potassium and aspartame – are added to the beverage in excess so that they provide a lovely sweetness without adding to the calorie intake. Although this duo of added sugars will not make Coke Zero sweet anymore, it definitely makes sense to be the chosen option among others who would stop from excessive consumption of sugars.

Coke not only envisages but purely executes the use of aspartame and acesulfame potassium as the perfect combination in its quest to remain uncontested in the beverage industry. As an icing on the cake this sweetening era is the proof of the logo's continuous research on providing a satisfying drink which also takes into account changing demands, even those related to fitness.

*Social Responsibility and Sustainability*

Tastes of Coca-Cola Zero's reduced sugar is not only the star seller, but also leaves sustainability and social obligation, too. The Coca-Cola Company realized enormous progress, along with the sustainable harvesting of ingredients, after the green packaging usage. The environmental burden was reduced. These pledges are in harmony with the mindsets of consumers who are not only concerned with but also zealous about environmentalism and look for manufacturers who are looking forward to safeguarding the environment.

Thus, Coca-Cola Zero does not only value the nutrition of its individual customers but also reflects the company's responsiveness to societal needs at a given moment. Apart from being the main visual cue of Coca-Cola Zero, its green color is referring to the ecologically minded consumers, who would for these brands that care about environment, adding Novelty to the market, where sustainability becomes more prominent. Social duty and sustainability are such corporate citizenship and environmental stewardship constituents as at Zero Coke mission one of its focuses is addressed. The brand, being an active player in the beverage industry, strongly believes in the necessity to reduce its environmental impact and to make targeted contributions to the sustainable development purposes. Not only does zero coke embrace ecology in its logo, but also manifests ecologically friendly practices throughout its whole supply chain. This is what is involved; which is the activities that are tailored to decrease emission of greenhouse gasses, make optimal use of energy, and ensure sustainable packaging measures. As an example, the implementation of renewable electricity resources like wind or solar energy at the production sites of Zero Coke has helped to reduce the necessity of fossil fuels and thus mitigate all the environmental harm that such fuels cause. In addition, the company Zero Coke puts great attention to buy the raw materials for its product from an environmentally friendly source. In this regard, we work together with our suppliers to ensure the farming methods are sustainable (the use of chemicals such as pesticides and fertilizers are kept to the minimum, landscapes are protected, and water is used and managed sparingly). A key goal of Zero Coke is to embrace the practice of sustainable sourcing not only to minimize its own carbon footprint but also to ensure the survival of agriculture and biodiversity in the future.

In fact there is also the other side that is all Zero Coke promotes as social responsibility and community involvement efforts. It includes all the charitable activities, be they the support of education, healthcare, and financial aid, that are essential in the development of local communities. Along with zeroing coke, humanizing its diversity and inclusion in the workers team of hires and the working condition is its main priority. It also supports equality and the empowerment of women.

However, Zero Coke tissue exchange and declarative talk with stakeholders to build support, belief, and accountability. This concerns regular disclosure of records showing its involvement with environmental and social problems, as well as that workers are being included in discussions and consultations and contracting in industry sustainability projects and partnerships.

## *Competitive Landscape*

Plain Coke, a sugar-free version of the conventional Coca-Cola, is challenging in a fast-paced and melodious environment within the beverage. By means of a market trend analysis, we account for core elements, such as market players, customer needs, and challenges.

Market Trends:

Zero Coke is in competition with the whole sugary-bearing drinks and those little-calorie in order to help fitness and health concerns develop. While paying attention to sugar consumption and its role in the prevention of lifestyle-associated health issues, the gap is being filled with zero-calorie sodas, the demand for which has substantially increased. Better than soda drinkers began to search for brands where they could enjoy the taste without worrying about the impact on their health. This kind of situation formed an ideal environment for products like Zero Coke.

## *Target audience and Marketing Strategies*

The beverage was remade by Coca-Cola, as consumers have become more health protective technology in the dynamic market of consumer choices and black-and-yellow industry. Like its fee-free counterpart, Zero Coke is a substitute, which is interesting for the vast many of customers who want to stay both healthy and with a zebra stripe on their cheek – not a lollipop.

Healthy-minded human beings from millennials to generation Z who are more cost-conscious and make better health-conscious nutritional options are Zero Coke's foremost niche market. This is to demonstrate that excessive consumption of sugar-laden mark beverages can lead to weight gain, raise risk of diabetes and obesity diseases and other lifestyle related diseases such as cardiovascular disease.

Through their connections to people who want to live actively and stay fit, the subgroup of the target audience – namely energetic lifestylers and health eaters – is the crucial part. As Zero Coke follows the dietary preferences of those who are dedicated to a regular active lifestyle, its global zero sugar recipe serves as a guidepost for products utilizing this trend. The audiences are usually in a lookout for a guilt-free answer that helps in keeping nature in addition to a flavorful drink. Coca-cola directs their market where health flavors are recognized and fitness goals and objectives are achieved with promoting Zero Coke as the preferred beverage of health conscious people who need to cut down on calories.

Besides this, Zero Coke targets children that belong to socially aware and techy groups of people. The online channels of information are in need for Generation Z and millennials, who are knowledgeable about the dietary value of the products they buy and pay for. The marketing approach for the duo 'Zero Coke' can capitalize on social media structures and internet standards which will have them directly connect to the demographic of youth and discuss its zero-calorie ingredients along with being sugar-free. The provision of transparency through true and sincere communication of products enhances the belief that the consumer has in them.

Moreover, the user base we aim for consists of mothers and fathers who are concerned about the nutrition of their children and who are health-conscious. Due to the increasing prevalence of childhood weight problems, parents strive to find sugar-free beverages as youngsters no longer drink sodas. This sugar-free recipe combined with its well-known and favorite Coca-Cola taste, Zero Coke could possibly be the one while they start helping their kids to inculcate the right habit at an earlier age. The diet-conscious consumers, another main target group of the soft drink giant, may also be attracted by Zero Coke as a family-friendly option that features its taste appealing to all groups of people, including children, and its sugarless nature.

But it should be mentioned right here that not everyone has the same nutritional dreams. So, these people who are fighting against diabetes or reducing the sugar in their diet make Zero Coke appealing to them. At this section of the portions of the real market, products which perfectly fit general needs while maintaining fine tastes are favored. People who desire affordable necessities found in this area of the market. Coca-Cola likewise could proceed with any Zero Coke as a healthful possibility for dieting minds via advertising its value as a sugar-free alternative that is useful for people with special health issues.

Furthermore, there is no need to deal with country limits as the ultimate market for Zero Coke is beyond counties. The drink is aimed at excellent consumers throughout the entire world in their quest for a refreshing alternative that carries healthy aspects, doing so in an increasingly globalized world where wellbeing and health developments defy cultural barriers. If a sky-brushed scenario would be relied on in which the cultural sensitivity-aware messaging that spotlights beauty of sugar-free Coca-Cola regardless of the place applied, the tagline 'Zero Coke - the choice of the ones who cherish them even the world over' may be portrayed.

Marketing strategies that helped gain effective target number were:


1. Product Positioning and Differentiation:

Coca-Cola Zero seeks to hook calorie-conscious consumers by strategically putting the product next to the everyday Coke ones.  This is an appealing option for calorie-conscious consumers with no added sugar. The main appeal in a competitive edge is the absence of sugar, and it would pull in those who choose coca Cola to taste no added sugar. The quote "Taste the Feeling," which has been adopted as the slogan of Zero Coke, is a first-rate marketing manifesto that efficiently conveys the brand's important characteristics and creates an emotional association with customers. These three words not only state the purpose of the brand but also capture the experience of cashing out but without the baggage of the Coke price in the most simple and yet memorable way. First of all "Taste the Feeling" tagline is dedicated to raising the flag of delivering a great beverage flavor that is tasty as well as fun. Sensational indulgence tagline took it one step forward with satisfaction - an image which appeals to clients' taste buds for wider interest. The implication is that Coke… Zero is as equally incredible as the original Coke and therefore the consumers getto enjoy the great flavor of their drink and without the guilt of consuming calories. The continuing movement of the market towards taste corresponds with premium offerings for products of tasteful character and superior character. Furthermore, with the slogan "Taste the Feeling" the brand unlocks its emotional resonance which is so much connected to Coca-Cola trademark and sound which is so dear to many consumers.


Coca Cola is closely associated with happiness, enjoyment or celebration.  This is what makes a product attribute. It is through these acts that the product itself becomes an inherent part of people's happiness. With the phrase "feeling" Zero Coke brings into mind the positive emotions of joy, happiness and connection" which have become the emblem of the Coca Cola logo. Emotional attachment to the brand through this resonance creates consumer loyalty and brand associations which then trigger their purchase of Zero Coke as their preferred drink brand. On the other hand, the tagline "Drink the Feeling" does not only play but it can also be a powerful, adaptable device for future campaigns. The advertising strategy involved using both the traditional advertising platforms for example television commercials, print ads and the virtual advertising systems such as social media and online content. The tagline therefore created a cohesive message which had a great impact on Zero Coke's brand recognition. It gives a brand the leverage of similar acts of relaying across diverse touchpoints to establish one identity that always stays atthe focal point of customers' perception. Additionally, not only is the tagline "Taste the Feeling", but is also an encouragement to interact with the product on a mental as well as emotional level. Imitating a slogan of the rival brand, "Make the taste", Zero Coke seduces the purchasers to "flavor" the effect and take part in the product experience, thereby shaping the emotional links. This interactive element offers a platform for customers to follow along and participate. This helps boost viewer interaction, which results in brand engagement and loyalty.

2. Target Market Segmentation:

Coca-Cola zero was designed for a particular group of people, namely, those who keep their health and who are the ones who are watchful of the sugar in their diet. Yet, they are still the ones who are ever curious about the remaining traditional taste of Coca-Cola. Axing this segment of the marketplace, comprising the teens and professionals who desire to lead a life of health but should not adopt the one of luxury, is the main target of the marketing campaigns.

3. Social Media Presence and Digital Marketing:

Coca-Cola Zero has focused heavily on social media marketing and digital channels, therefore it catches everyone's attention. To reach the young men and women, we use campaigns with interactive forms, influencers collaborations as well as interesting fabric can be applied. Through the media networks system, consumers can share their experiences on how refreshing coca-cola zero is, which therefore spreads the brand's name among their social connections.

4. Collaborations and Partnerships:

To widen its reach, Coca-Cola Zero signature brand of strategic alliance and partnership with some of the companies is an important step. Joining up with fun and adventurous sport events, or becoming an active participant of events that are major in your area enable the brand to be vibrant and zesty. Building relationships with saw-practicing experts and influencers inherit the fame of the brand and its credibility.

5. Innovative Design and Packaging:

Coca-Cola Zero's packaging clearly pursues a purpose of simplicity and attractive design of today. Its black packaging intentionally works together with the zero-calorie idea as well as a sugar-free feature that is different from the average red Coca-Cola cans. What is more, the package has got an eye-catching objective and arrangement that gives it the first top position.

6. Sampling and Experiential Marketing:

The sampling of Coke Zero is a potent strategy to let the customers taste the product before they make it up their mind. These types of activities are most often on bustling streets, popular gatherings and by arrangement with merchants. Coca-Cola by providing samples to customers will build a bond between clients and the brand and help them shift from more traditional sodas to Coca-Cola Zero.

7. Health and wellbeing projects:

Coca-Cola Zero's marketing strategy is based on the fact that the product plays an important role in a lifestyle centered on fitness and health through various health and fitness tasks. In the advertisement campaign that runs constantly, the idea of consuming a delicious beverage and staying fit without compromise is further supported because most ad material talks about the beverage's low sugar and calorie content.

8. Global Consistency with Local Adaptations:

Coca-Cola Zero stores its advertising procedures closer to the community in order to cater to the taste and cultural quirks of those localities, but maintains the international picture of its brand at the same time. This technique protects Lara's original message of indulging in a sugar-free healthy beverage that can engage the diverse audience around the world.

*Customer Feedback*

Zero Coke, which is a sugar-free version of the soda, has been catching the market's eye, no matter being a newcomer to the beverage market. To ensure this particular product's successful and client's satisfaction, it is critical to continually check the feedback from the clients. This article looks into the punter expressions, revealing their perspectives, problems, and advice concerning the absence of Coke.

Positive Feedback:

The excellent feedback for Zero Coke, in general, revolves around its sugar-free formula and the taste of regular Coke, identical to original Coca-Cola. People are moved by the brand's loyalty in creating a healthier option which doesn't affect the unwavering taste. For numerous customers, the newly introduced product is an epitomized replication of the original flavor without the unneeded energy, thus an appealing desire for the ones who look for options to cut down on their sugar intake.

Moreover, Coca-Cola customers praise the company for the sport and health consideration aspect which they have created to attract the wellness-focused segment of the society. The 0-calorie part has become the favorite element by the people, attracting healthy consumers to try the product.

Consumer Perceptions:

The analysis of customer feelings is of paramount importance in determining the general population's response towards the Coke Zero. The customers most often say that the company's products are closely connected with a good and healthy lifestyle, which is its key to success. Customers associate Zero Coke as a sugar-free delight which allows them to indulge in the taste of Coca-Cola without its health downsides such as overeating.

While, some customers might have raised particular concerns with artificial sweeteners used in Zero Coke, thereby attracting questions to do with their health impact. Health concerns alongside act as decisive tangible factors in shaping the customers' view of the Zero Coke product. Increasingly a number of health concerns with regard to sugar intake and obesity are moving more and more consumers to view zero coke as a healthier alternative to a regular soda. The lack of sugar or calories in Zero Coke complies with the fitness-oriented consumers alternatives that favor this beverage, assuming that you are trying to lessen the level of sugar intake or simply following a healthy diet routine. While this raises a positive part in terms of increased sales, some of the purchasers might have objections about using artificial sweeteners in Zero Coke, which will cause the problem of fitness risks or side effects that might be associated with them. The perceptions imply that Coca-Cola needs to be more transparent to consumers by showing that it conforms to safety guidelines and industry regulations as it pertains to the ingredients within the product.

*Challenges and Concerns*

Despite the fact that service quality is generally positive, the customer commentary leads to positive problems or something that deserves even higher praise. A fascinating thing is the artificial sweetener aftertaste; it is less attractive to a certain group of people instead of the original product. This is a problem that needs to be tackled in order to upstage the pride of customers and in the long run engender product loyalty.

Another objective is to engage in conflicts with the sugar-free or low-calorie liquids already in the market. Consumers are annoyingly comparing Zero Coke to competing products, which is a quality of an impeccably dynamic market, and reinforcing the necessity of never ending development and innovation.

Suggestions and Improvements:

Customer feedback is the priceless hint both to the removable areas of the improvement and to the improvements themselves in Zero Coke's performance. Opinions involve creation of different flavoring options in order to cover people's different tastes, improvement of marketing strategies to highlight unique benefits and addressing concerns about aftertaste through reformulation or use of alternative sweeteners.

Besides, they tend to prefer environmentally friendly packaging made with sustainable materials, which is evident of their awareness of the environmental footprint. Introducing eco-conscious products within the product's lifecycle would provide aesthetic added values with ecologically aware consumers.

We were able to understand the perspectives of customers by analyzing the remarks from Zero Coke, which clearly gives hints of hurdles, worries, and opportunities. The products never come under the scanner due to its success rate to provide sugar-free Cola to the consumers without the undesirable taste. On the one hand, overcoming challenges of resemblance and artificial sweeteners are of paramount concern to consumer satisfaction.

Apart from that, the recommendations from the consumers turn into future maps for the enhanced versions and innovations, hence, Zero Coke is always a superior and demanded option in the ever- changing channels. Emphasizing on customer feedback and continual improvement of the product will help Zero Coke to achieve the honorable status among other competitors in the market segment of sugar- free drinks.


## *Sales Performance*

Having Xero Coke, which is a calories and sugar-free beverage, gained so much popularity because healthy choices now are everyone's obsession that people are beginning to choose sugar-free sodas over typical ones. The analysis here pertains to Zero Coke total income and how external and internal elements have been playing in achieving this goal.

Market Trends and Consumer Preferences

The move generally towards a healthier lifestyle has increased client demand for products incorporating lesser sugar amounts.

Ashley's lyrics create a unique, energetic atmosphere that is a prime example of the cultural impact of music in our society. The no Coke alternative pioneers itself not only as a delicious but also healthy soft drink relevant to the athletic people and those who try to maintain their body weight. The appropriation of healthy lifestyle style definitely is the one of the factors leaving a brand as the market leader.

Product Innovation and Marketing Strategies

A critical factor that has cemented the excellent market performance for Zero Coke is the brand's consistent push for new product innovation. The creation of new tastes, better formulations, smart marketing and advertising campaigns made the brand continue to evolve to gain wider recognition from the different consumers. Many collaborations and partnerships with influencers, fitness specialists and advocates of health have also performed a significant role in creating brand name awareness and influencing buying decisions.

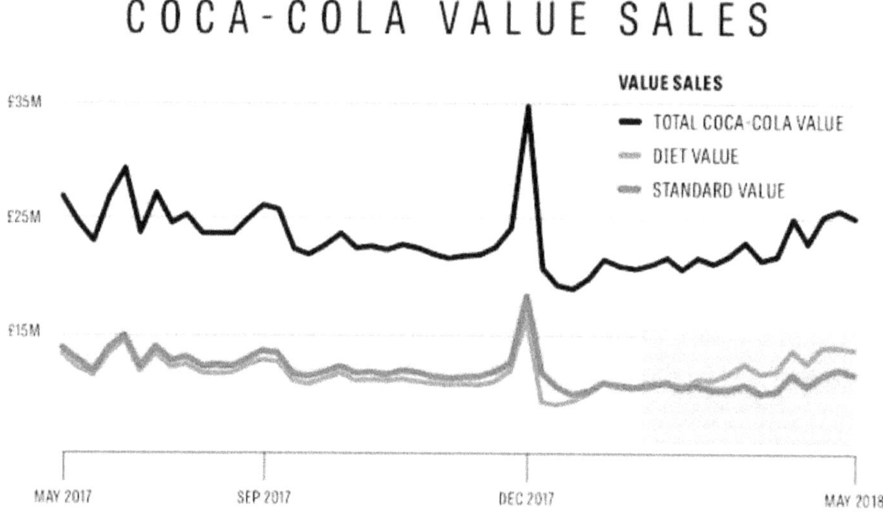


Distribution Channels and Accessibility

In fact, within the scope of various channels of distribution getting Zero Coke has become the major factor for sales performance. The product's placement in local supermarkets, comfort stores, web based platforms and vending machines, make it simple to find and purchase it by the customers. In an effort to increase the number of distribution points, we have successfully expanded our distribution community that has in turn pushed for more marketplace penetration and resulting in growth of income figures as a whole. Snack products distribution strategy is greatly contributed by its huge network of retail partners, including convenience stores, comfort shops and supermarkets.

Through this partnership those gateways are reflected to the consumers wherever they go during their normal shopping behavior. Besides, for Zero Coke, wholesalers and beverage vendors form durable partnerships, with one of the primary responsibilities of these deals being prompt and widespread distribution to stores throughout the country. This multiple distribution channel increases the popularity and ensures that the merchandise is always in our custody and is available to the customers on time. In addition, the brand focuses on accessibility through increasing store installations across alternative retail networks. Among these are the merchandising processes, fuel stations and shopping via online platforms. Actions by the important introduction of vending machines which will offer an immediate access to Zero Coke products in heavily trafficked locations like airports, transport stations and office buildings to customers who are very busy.

The gas stations are no less important as they form a network of the distribution channel through which the distributors sell the Zero Coke products to the consumers as they also refill their vehicles. More importantly, many on-line platforms being the distributors for Zero Coke in addition make it very accessible, and customers need only to press a button in order to have their favored Zero Coke products brought to their doorstep. Besides, the strategy also incorporates shipping containers around the world. With the aid of cashing upon its distinct distribution capacity for its sister enterprise, Coke, Zero Coke products can be found in many countries across the world. Such an international presence makes it possible that the clients from anywhere in the world could ever purchase from Zero Coke, even if they are in another country. As an international player, Zero Coke benefits from the global market access and thus from the expansion of its customer segment as the one of the largest players of the beverage industry.

Furthermore, Zero Coke incorporates modern distribution techniques making the products not only eligible but also on the other hand which meet the changing expectations of the customers. These include food transport services together with subscription base models, which enables customers to enjoy Zero Coke merchandise through delivery amenities. Consuming new traits and learning classical products during the changing patron patterns and alternative of the product Zero Coke maintains it on the hands and at ease in the rapid market.

Competitive Landscape

An evaluation of Zero-Coke's overall performance finds a need to consider the competitive environment surrounding the beverages industry. Brand's ability to create an identifiable and measurable distance from the competition through its significant promotion proposition (USP) is what has granted it an edge upon many players in the same market. By following frequent market trends and creating designs that do not waste time in making the consumer's choice possible, Zero Coke has always been ahead of the competition. As the intensively competitive field of the beverage industry, where Zero Coke is the leading player in the zero-calorie sodas category, emerges as one of the frontrunners. The 2 main competitors of Coca-Cola are other beverage producers introducing sugar-free alternatives on the market, such as Pepsi Co's Pepsi Zero Sugar and Diet Pepsi and Dr. Pepper Snapple Group's Diet Dr Pepper. Competitors such as these creates challenges to the market domain of Zero Coke that brand recognition, the distribution networks, and the marketing approaches of them to pose problems to it and also capture the market share. Second, up-and-coming brands in the health and wellness beverage sector which consist of sparkling water makes such as LaCroix and Bubly are also others plus alternatives for people who are having a craving for low-calorie beverages. A very important step that Zero Coke takes to be distinct and stand apart from competitors is a strong connection to Coca-Cola logo, novel flavors and vigorous brand campaigns.

The startup of this new product achieves this goal by constantly innovating and adapting to vibrant consumer desires, placing it in a competitive position within the market as it navigates the varied waters of this prosperous competitive beverage industry.

Economic Factors and Price Sensitivity

Economic situations and habits of consumers pay an equally crucial part in boosting the sales performance. With Coke Zero pricing tactics, however, healthy beverage alternatives will be in the light of day while price-sensitive people will be keen to buy, though the profitability will be a factor to consider since people will only buy if they are price-conscious. Undertaking sales statistics review relative to an economic report allows for the creation of valuable insights on the stimulating effect that external factors have on a brand overall performance.

Regulatory Compliance and Health Trends

With fitness regulations being brought in as standards, compliance will finally matter in the case of the operational review of the income performance. The ideational affinity of Coke Zero with fitness and security environment is a basic element in building endorsement with consumers. Forecasting health concerns earlier and adapting the products duly for the changing consumer tastes might equally translate to better revenue.

Major Players

The key players within the low calorie soda sector are big shots companies for instance Coca -Cola, PepsiCo, and Dr Pepper Snapple Group. Zero Coke, the newcomer from Coca-Cola, is going to enter the same market segment as PepsiCo's Pepsi Zero Sugar and Diet Coke and the competitors are there to welcome them.

Every producer applies advantageous marketing and advertising efforts to create their product unique and conquer a bigger share of the market. Using their big brand present-day status and large distribution channel as their ace, these companies are consolidating the market. The Zero Coke from the Coca-Cola Company's inventory, however, deviates from competitors in the market with its branding, tasty flavor, and marketing tactics. For example, the branding and associations with Coca-cola are among the major marketing strategies used by this product. The world knows the charismatic coke brand as one that grants happiness from within.

Over time, the Coca-Cola marketers has become a true industry leader due to its marketing skills and influence across the globe. Their brand name is associated with the original Coca-Cola products, and this gives Zero-Coke a lot of attention from customers, hence, it is recognized as a natural extension of the main Coca-Cola brand.

While the main point that puts Zero Coke ahead of its competition is its flavor, there are other characteristics that make Zero Coke stand out against other drinks in the market. Zero Coke provides a sugar conscious alternative to Coca-Cola, the conventional drink that contains high levels of sugar, catering to clients who want to cut down on their sugar consumption without giving up on its sensory appeal. Unsweetened Coke is a copycat of the original Coca-Cola product, replicating the same taste. When buyers consume it, familiar flavor and satisfaction are associated with it. Flavor of this product is what sets it apart from other fizzy no-sugar sodas that are available commercially, many which may be chemical-flavored or leave an odd aftertaste in the mouth. Offering consumers a no-sugar-added drink that in no way compromises on the taste and still manages to fit the bill as a healthy product is what makesthis new product line Zero Coke stand out from the rest and move towards a very dominant position in themarket.

Besides branding and taste, how Zero Coke's advertising strategies help it to be distinctive are worth mentioning. By zero coke, Coca-cola puts its constant effort in terms of the innovative and engaging advertising campaigns, and it could be said that this is not an exception. A synergy between traditional advertising methods (e. g. , television and print media) and online platforms (like social media and virtual media) Zero Coke maintains a spirit-consuming advertising that captures the minds of consumers. A style of logo frequently works with celebrities, influencers and sports organizations to create discussions and excitement about merchandize releases. Such marketing activities that are inspired to reach the peak of mind and lead to the increasing impact of Zero Coke on becoming the number one option for the consumption of those who have had enough of sugar in soda.

Moreover, Zero Coke falls into a unique place through pursuing trendy consumer choices and innovative development. Furthermore, fitness and specialized beverages have become more and more vital areas to consumers as concerns about health and wellness continue to gain traction around the globe. This has, therefore, not only enabled Zero Coke to develop new brands and versions but, more importantly, to evolve itself to the changing conditions. For example, the logo creatively offers only seasonal drinks and special diet products targeted to different demographics including athletes and diet health-aware people. An agile model of customer service, mindful of the customers feedback, and a wide distribution facilitates Zero Coke's rapid growth in the competitive market environment. To sum up, our drink, Zero Coke, is different from competitors not only through strong branding and unique taste but also due to impressive ad campaigns and a wide consumer-base. Using the popularity and a historical background of the Coke emblem and proposing a sugar-free choice that doesn't sacrifice on the taste, Zero Coke has positioned itself a no match in the corporations league. Considering the wide array of clients' options is what has made Zero Coke leave no room to recede from the race for the mouth-watering needs of a greatly diverse and sophisticated population.

Consumer Preferences

Understanding patron options is critical for Zero Coke's success. Consumers are more and more health-conscious, in search of merchandise with herbal ingredients, zero-calorie content material, and no synthetic sweeteners. Additionally, the call for eco-friendly packaging and sustainable practices is developing. Zero Coke, together with other foremost gamers, desires to continuously adapt to these converting alternatives by innovating their product formulations and packaging strategies to fulfill patronexpectancies.

Innovation and Product Development

The beverage industry in general goes in for continuous innovation, therefore companies put a lot of money into research and developments to create new and more modern formulations. Recall a time when still in school, they had to run up and down all day long or carry heavy books without a break, so they learned how to plan ahead. Instead of producing a stale tasting beverage, they could turn to innovative sweeteners or plant-based flavorings to enhance their product line. Progress would be embodied in advancing technologies and ability to follow trends, will certainly safely land us in the zone of the leading group. A crucial breakthrough point has been the flavor availability and new product variants that offer numerous taste choices to additives and an option to spoil the consumers. In addition to the authentic version of Zero Coke, other variations have been released, such as the zero calorie cherry, vanilla and orange vanilla Zero Cokes. They are also sugar free and different, giving them an innovative aspect to appeal to their customer base. With regard to packaging, the company has accomplished package design and certain benefits by which this product has been beautified. The emergence skukani to kansho cans, resealable bottles, and on-the-cross packaging directory embodies Zer0 Coke's adduce consumer's needs for comfortable and easy to carry beverage services. In addition its efforts in addition to this a percentage of the carbonate is investing in sustainable packaging tasks like lightweighting bottles. It is also uses recycled substances and tries to create opportunities of alternative packaging materials in order to mitigate the environmental effects and recycling efforts. The development and product improvement initiatives of Zero Coke has been directed towards an expansion of the taste options, to achieving a more sustainable packaging system, applying user-oriented solutions to achieve brand loyalty, as well as placing a premium on health and fitness values through the ingredient innovation. Leading the way in consumer trends and possibilities , Zero Coke always stays ahead and a yearly leader within the 0-calorie beverage category precisely because it provides the newest refreshments solutions which excite customers all over the world.

Distribution Channels

A reliable distribution system is necessary for the accomplishment of diet beverages having zero calories. Major companies utilize their distribution channels widely to ensure that their products are always reachable on shop shelves, convenience stores and grocery shops. Making strategic alliances with distributors and retailers can greatly help Zero Coke hold the high shelf area and add a massive number of supporters.

Marketing and Branding

Marketing and branding are of paramount importance for making consumers' mindset. The approach of Zero Coke is strongly based on effective marketing campaigns, social media involvement and the cooperation with important fitness and wellbeing institutions. This market abounds in brand loyalty, therefore, creating a remarkable brand picture through open conversation about materials and health benefits is imperative.

Regulatory Challenges

The beverage industry is challenged in attorneyship, especially with regard to fitness claims, labeling, and element regulations. In the same way as Zero Coke needs to abide by those regulations in order to be compliant even though having the appealing product. Staying abreast of a dynamic regulatory environment and future-proofing the business by adapting to the changes is a key component of long-term success.

Global Expansion

The company "Zero Coke" works in one of the most unstable markets, where buyers have multiple choices, regulatory aspects differ, and cultural barriers arise. Balancing regional specificities with consistency of brand image and achieving that through product and advertising modifications is not an easy task. The increase of the market share worldwide demands to be culturally perceptive and ideally ready to serve different market segments.


Consequently, Coke operates within a field which is surrounded by and competitive with all contenders while being in the sugar-free beverage market. To stabilize and prosper, employment must engage in innovation, link the demands of the customer with the product, invest in efficient distribution networks and skillfully navigate through the layered regulatory frameworks. While strategic advertising and international expansion are two key levers in this booming method, different customer insights and mobility make it more tricky entering the market environment. The organization must conform to conserve, still be adaptive to new trends and foresight long-term success being its ultimate aim.

### *Challenges and Successes*

The operation of the beverages industry has undergone a significant paradigm shift over recent years due to the changing customers' attitude, health concerns, and environmental issues. An avoidable effect is that a number of the popular drinks will be redesigned or created without calories, such as Zero Coke. Zero Coke is not a conventional situation, the assessment that follows encompasses the pros and the cons which Zero Coke has faced with this dynamic landscape.

Challenges:

- Health Concerns and Perception: From the beginning, one of the main tasks for Zero Coke is trying to help with the worries about health related to artificial sweeteners. Though they are believed to be sugar-alike, the call to use sweeteners like aspartame and sucralose has left many tongues wagging as to their long-term health consequences. And besides that, some customers think of these blocks as weird and gaudy, that ruins the first impression of Zero The Coke.

- Competitive Market: The beverage industry lays a pretty tough competing field, as there is so much choice and the customer interest fluctuates. The tough competition that I face with other diet sodas is no longer presented as a single enemy but also from a growing range of health drink alternatives such as the natural juice, flavored water, and the functional liquids. It's very challenging to bring the message to the public while staying unique and creative in the advertising space.
- Consumer Education: Besides the marketing communication channel, the process of letting the target audience know how Zero Coke's no-sugar contributes to their health also should be well designed. With wrong notions about artificial sweeteners and most consumers not knowing how to check the dietary allegations on Zero Coke, the product cannot be accepted. Definitely this is a known effort that includes the focus on promotion, advertisement, and clear description by highlighting the product features.
- Sustainability Concerns: While in the environment focused world the distributionally as well as production aspects for Zero Coke will also undergo an additional examination. Maximum care should be taken to reduce the carbon footprint by minimizing manufacturing and disposal requirements as well the environmental impact caused by the recyclability or non-recyclability of packaging materials. The sustainability risk will be mirrored at the fact of its long epoch.


Successes:

- Health-Conscious Consumer Base: The newest and first of its kind, Zero Coke brand has targeted the consumers who are leaning towards a healthier alternative. As people start watching their sugar consumption and calorie intake more, the 0 calorie per serve or calorie-free element of the Zero Coke starts to appear as an irresistible offer. The brand has achieved a greater degree of product differentiation whilst maintaining the notion that it was a healthier alternative to a normal soda.
- Innovation in Flavor Varieties: Just to keep the patron interest, Zero Coke has selected to venture into innovation in such a way that it creates different types of flavors. This is a range of choices such as a cherry zero coke with vanilla and lime zest, which are options of cherry, vanilla and lime spices targeted to diversified preferences. This switch has been conducted not just to enrich the in-house variety but also to bring in clients who are looking for specificity and individualization of their coffee experience.

- Strategic Marketing Campaigns: Coke Zero has had to confront the troubles of its customers in promoting the image brands and create their market fidelity. Open communication about no-sugars, not too many calories and no harmful side effects is key to fair perception of this item. The comment section below the corresponding classified ads reinforces the symbol's loyal participation in the health and taste factor, which the audience has been confirming.
- Global Reach and Brand Recognition: Presence of Coca-Cola in an international scene in addition to the implementation of the Zero Coke policy has had a noble impact so far. Users of the Zero Coke can also choose emblem designs sourced directly from the highly recognized and widely distributed community of fashion creatives. Being the long-established trademark of Coca-Cola, the company has a solid opportunity to break into markets and get consumer consideration through its famous soda Zero Coke. Zero Coke's venture in the beverage industry, which took place in the dynamic scenario, was hugely guided by the various challenges and successes faced. However, the brand marks not only as a response to health concerns but also as the demonstration of innovative tactics and strong marketing strategy. Yet the brand should deal with challenges linked to the market competition, client perception, and the sustainability aspect. The evolutionary development of clients choices and the business ambience necessitate periodical adaptation and creativity if no coke is to survive in the coming years. As the beverage space changes rapidly, the ability of the logo to meet those new challenges and build on existing achievements will determine its position and reputation both on the national and global brands.

***Other Products by Coca-Cola***

Consumers nowadays are more aware and have different inclinations that are all focusing on healthy diet hence an increased demand for healthy beverage options such as juices, teas and functional drinks of this type. Coca-Cola is precisely looking to be a part of the non-carbonated categories to amplify its market share and tap into the emerging sections of the market with a significant growth potential so as to satisfy the growing consumer tastes.

1. Minute Maid (1960):

Coca-Cola produces Minute Maid which is the main maker of fruit juices and other non-carbonated drinks since they made the acquisition of it in 1960. The Minute brand helped Coca-Cola to make use of the juice category and therefore took the opportunity at increasing demand for fruit-based beverages.

2. Dasani (1999):

Coca-Cola created the Dasani brand in 1999 with an intention to have access to non-carbonated water which is different from the central business. In just a few years, Dasani Kwik was able to achieve the major position regarding the supply of bottled water in the United States. regarding the Coca-Cola distribution system as well as through the voice of the product without any prejudice (positive and only the positive).

3. Honesty Tea (2011):

In pursuit of sustainable prosperity and declining soft drink consumption, Coca-Cola purchased Honest Tea, a healthier and naturally crafted beverage, in 2011. This was to broaden the company's product variety in order to cater for the expanding market for organic and natural foods. Honest Tea was donatedby Coca-Cola in this regard to target new consumers who preferred healthy and eco-friendly drinks as theones with sweet syrups.

4. Ice (2007):

Coca-Cola sold its series of vitamin water and smart water brands to Glacy when it started to create advanced waters, which tapped into the functional water beverages category. Coca-Cola has gained extensive footprints in the emerging market- which has given high growth potential to the functionaldrinks and high premium water, with the acquisition of Glasio.

5. Costa Coffee (2018):

In 2018 Coca-Cola acquired Costa Coffee which is one of international's biggest coffee chains, thus accessing the global coffee market. By successfully purchasing Costa Coffee and stabilizing its footinginside the coffee segment, Coca-Cola now offers more than just refreshments.


*Impact and Future Outlook*

- Revenue Diversification and Growth Opportunities:1. Revenue Diversification and Growth Opportunities: Due to Coca-Cola's entry into all non-carbonated drinks, this has made the company diversify its major products line and to exploit the opportunity in new and growing beverage categories. Nowadays, non-carbonated drinks comprise a crucial segment of Coca-Cola Sales' revenue and have become a main growth driver in the company's growing trend.

- Consumer Engagement and Brand Loyalty: By offering a broad range of beverages, Coca-Cola has the ability to reach consumers in the distinct segments of the market, as well as reinforce brand fidelity in tying the product's innovation and personalization. Besides that, Coca-Cola is also able to attract health-aware consumers who choose the non-carbonated beverages which are more natural and healthier drink choices.
- Innovation and Sustainability: Coca-Cola not only expands its reach into non-carbonated beverages but also improves the product line by way of new varieties, packaging options and a growing concern for consumers and the environment. Periodically an attentive and creative Company will make modifications. The organization's sustainability and environmental management services spread beyond its carbonated beverages business to include projects designed to minimize plastic waste and carbon pollution. Therefore, car launches for such projects are a must for success.

Through the diversification strategies in non-carbonated drinks, Coca-Cola clearly showcases the company's focus on innovation and building long-term stakes. By adopting varieties of strategist, this company has been able to product beyond waters, and serve the global beverage industry with consumers and investors.

**Branding and marketing strategies for Coca-Cola's diversified product portfolio**

Coca-Cola, a multinational leader in beverage making, has over the years massively widened its product variety from the traditional carbonated drinks. Now, there are various types of drinks like water, juice, tea, sports drinks in the portfolio. In this tie up, the agency will be exploiting its logo as an emblem, adapting to the consumer wants by repositioning its products, and introducing different drinks in its product portfolio.

<h2 style="text-align:center">Corporate Social Responsibility and Sustainability</h2>

The responsibility of corporate citizenship (CCRS) and sustainability in the economic activities of Coca-Cola are now becoming critical organizational activities which signify the firm's devotion to environmental stewardship, social impact, and ethics disclosure. With a history of helping the community that dates back to the company's early years, that is, Dr. John Pemberton who had a share of the Coca-Cola's sales being donated  to charity. As time passes by, Coca-Cola acts as a patron to many philanthropic programs such as scholarships, disaster aid efforts and community improvement projects. Over the past two decades, Coca-Cola's surveys of its CSR activities have moved on from traditional philanthropy to encompass environmental sustainability, employee engagement and consumer engagement. The committee started examining linkages between social and environmental factors with that of the economic system of society.

*CSR Sacraments of Coca-Cola*

- Environmental Sustainability: Coca-Cola's main objective is to create the least impact on the environment throughout the whole production chain starting from the raw materials sources up to the production plant, distribution, and packaging. The utility will go farther and will set a goal of minimizing the amount of water usage, carbon discharge, as well as trash and will invest in advanced generation and sustainable measures.
- Community Engagement: Through task-based projects with partners that focus on education, health, water stewardship and in the economic response, Coca-Cola engages relevant sector groups. The human enterprise collaborates with other groups, community leaders and governments to overcome the socially disruptive situations and customize an experienced future.
- Ethical Business Practices: The Coca-Cola system is guided by ideas of transparency, accountability, and responsible governance. The company's principle is securing workers' safety,being diverse and respecting human rights in the global supply chain. Promoting genuine green practices is also its aim.

*CSR's Key Initiatives and Programs Of The Organization*

- Water Use: With the software for water management the aim happens to be the accent on water consumption and using production and water processes, water availability as well as ware availability are selling categories. The company taps local authorities and NGOs to work with them in building water refill stations in some areas where there's plenty of water supply around theglobe.

- Women Empowerment: Coca-Cola follows an approach which comprises three components: It promotes women employment, education, and career oriented development at all levels. Such steps of the neobank's 5 by 20 program allows empowering 5 million female salespeople of financial sector by the means of dedicated training, mentoring and access to sourcing
- New Applications and Packaging: Coke is introducing the packaging recycling experience and is also raising the recycled content amount in bottles and cans. The company has rolled out two packages such as "World Without Waste" and "PlantBottle" to refurbish recycling infrastructures and menswear sustainable packaging systems respectively.

*The Extent and Effect of Coca-Cola's Going CSR Program*

- Environmental Impact: Coca-Cola's holistic offers solutions to save badly needed water, to decrease greenhouse gas emission, and to cut down the production wastefully done for years. The company in question investments in renewable energy, green water technologies, and circular finance solutions has demonstrated the principles are very much beneficial in the environment.
- Social Impact: Coca-Cola's community engagement program based on its programs of skill improvement, health and wealth are responsible for the betterment of the lives of millions of people globally, majorly in the community development sectors. Community relations is facilitated by Coca-Cola's departments whose engagements with local business and government create an opportunity for school access sale, gym and fitness amenities development, and create an inclusive economy for the underserved.

*Uncertainties and direction for the Future*

- Sustainability goals: Coca-Cola is currently operating under a tightly constrained situation where its efforts in water consumption, which are certainly vital, plastic waste recovery and supply chains are instantly taken into consideration. The organization has to be passionate, innovator and collaborator by working with different stakeholders to tackle these challenges and continue with its way towards the sustainable development goals.
- Stakeholder contacts: Management skills are necessary for and making sure that Coca-Cola achieves its CSR objectives of commitment to stand for and associating with others will involve dialog and significant involvement by these people who care. Stakeholder engagement can be a sore challenge to Coca-Cola whose concern is getting stakeholders' feedback and dealing with issues, always adapting its CSR strategies to fit evolving expectations and goals.

*Environmental Efforts, Community Engagement Programs, and Philanthropic Activities*

Coca-Cola, being the major international brewery, has a good deal of effects on the atmosphere and population in places where it is carried out. Responding to its role as a responsible corporate citizen, Coca-Cola has carried out several projects on environmental and social philanthropy which are aimed at mitigating environmental degradation, continuing the community dialogue and the men, women and children are having better lives in the society. It also analyzes its deep philanthropy diatribe which is in terms of a scope, impact as well as it's important to the drivers of sustainable development and social responsibilities.

Environmental efforts

- Water Use: The Coca-Cola Company's strong corporate commitments on sustainability have been underpinned by decisions resulting from water management involving huge amounts of water consumption by its manufacturing sites. Coca-Cola intends to replenish its fluids by working with farmers in regions around the world to establish agricultural systems so that a reliable supply of natural water can be assured with the help of its "Replenish" program. Water efficiency has been integrated in the sector's agenda, and water conservation projects have been implemented regionally to areas affected by abnormal water scarcity.
- Packaging and recycling: Coca-Cola is fully dedicated to a sustainable future with cutting-edge packaging and recycling ventures. The company came up with concentrated efforts with the industrialization of technology machinery methods of improving, lightweight materials, recyclable materials as well as plant based bottles. Coca-Cola offers reusable packaging promotion and consumer training which is essential in increasing the recycling rates and reducing plastic waste.
- Weather action: By now, The entity Coca-Cola has established an objective for a global count of greenhouse gasses emissions that deals with operations at the factories, distribution and refrigerations. The organization makes investments in renewable energy, energy efficient technologies as well as carbon offset initiatives that are meant to contrive a small carbon footprint. Among the UN Framework Convention on Climate Change of Paris Agreement and the

international Program of science-based instruments, Coca-Cola has always been an active supporter.

Community participation programs

- Women Empowerment: Coca-Cola's 5by20 app seeks to enable almost 5 million young women around the globe to contribute through education, mentoring, and resources to economic growth. The work targets such sectors as agriculture, the retail trade, and the hospitality industry where for women the problem of economic participation is acute. Coca-Cola associates and NGOs, governments and groups will further implement 5by20 projects particularly at the international level.
- Youth Development: Coca Cola develops schemes for the youth which avail them education, employment and entrepreneurship. Here one can bubble ideas of youth leadership and create their own good future with possibilities of grants, vocational centers courses and job programs. Coca-Cola has a cooperative relation with the schools, universities and children groups in the target audience aimed at raising awareness and getting a hand of life skills as well career development.
- Health and Wellness: Activating the Coca-Cola future initiatives that will focus on promoting health and balance with programs that will promote active living, vitamin balance, and lifestyle choices that depict good health. The board teams up with public health organizations, sports committees and local ventures by sponsoring sport's events, fitness programmes and nutrition clubs at schools so as to reinforce meals of balanced diet. Coca-Cola Company instituted a strategy of responsible advertising and product innovation to minimize the sugar content and to provide health drinks.

Charity activities

- Disaster Relief: Through its Coca-Cola humanitarian and disaster relief initiatives, the company works as one big community that provides relief for citizens and people who suffer from catastrophic natural events or humanitarian crises. Employers give water, logistical assistance to aid agencies and affected communities to build their capacity and response in times when they need it. The scope of Coca-Cola's disaster relief efforts encompasses the provision of essential goods that will suffice short-term needs, reconstituting infrastructure, and strengthening long-term resilience.

- Educational Policies: Coca-Cola participates in the development of training methods that enhance early attainment, deepen educational influence, and let students in the higher levels of their education to transpire their dreams. By this measure, the college grants scholarships, improves faculty infrastructure, participates in teacher school teaching, and provides term–time services. Coca-Cola works in partnership with schools, NGOs and governments to solve relevant educational gaps by making learners know more of the offered products and attitudes for positive living.
- Community Development: Coca-Cola socialized things by starting programs of networking that help to tackle issues on social, economic and environmental level by the community. It invests in multi-agency collaborations with networks, water and sanitation facilities, infrastructure projects and capacity building initiatives. CocaCola and the partner network organizers as well as NGOs and decision-making bodies work together to address priorities of resource mobilization and sustainability. They use this approach to promote sustainable development projects.

Impact and consequences

- Environmental Impact: Coca-cola's environmental policies have created much lower consumption of water, much lower carbon emission and new technology towards the reduction of wastes. The water management and innovative packaging technologies embedded into the company's environmental practices are consistent with standard business operations. Coca-Cola's dedication to environmental sustainability builds brand image, lowers the operating expenses and controls the risks associated with the ecological destruction which in turn boosts the revenues and hence the profits.
- Social Impact: Beyond any words, Coca-Cola's community engagement can be seen to have transformed the lives of hundreds of thousands of people in the circle of influence through the advocacy and promotion of women empowerment, fitness and general well-being of the child. The organization may achieve far-reaching effects through its investments in social cohesion, education and disaster response in communities where such groups are disadvantaged. The philanthropic activities of Coca-Cola remind everyone that corporate citizenship matters, and thatbusiness can be a force for good and a participant in addressing the world's critical issues as an integral part of the society.

Controversies and Challenges

The brand's CSR programs, like any other, undoubtedly have their controversies and problems.

Coca-Cola being one of the leading MNC's in the beverage industry, it has its own share of social and economic responsibilities. Despite the company's constructive efforts towards promoting environmental responsibility, communication and business ethics, it still faces the criticism of stakeholders. In response to employee complaints and the investigations into their labor abuse, strategic marketing as well as the criminal litigation of human rights, this survey tries to uncover the multi-faceted sides of the question of what lies behind Coca-Cola's CSR activities besides wealth creation and possible reparation.

1. Environmental challenges

- Water use and pollution: Coca-Cola process is water intensive which insinuates that the company can exhaust water supplies and probably degrade the quality of water resources especially in areas that experience water shortages. This corporation is often blamed for contaminating the local groundwater sources by its pollution causing activities, which invariably leads to degradation of our water bodies and water shortage in the areas that they are located. At one point, Coca-Cola has been the target of criticism related to water bottling in the vicinity of natural areas, wild-life sanctuaries and water supplies of native aboriginal communities that use slushy water.

- Plastic pollution and waste management: Coca-Cola's use of plastic containers as a packaging material has led to massive environmental waste and plastic pollution in many parts of the country. Has directed criticisms towards the enterprise for manufacturing immense quantities of non-biodegradable plastics which subsequently accumulate into the marine ecosystem without sufficient measures such as recycling and disposal. Criticisms arise against Coca-Cola as it strives to set goals for the recycling of PET bottles and a sustainable packaging, as the people demand targets and specific actions in the plastic waste problem.

- Climate change and carbon emissions: However, the carbon footprint of Coca-Cola, specifically related to production, distribution and refrigeration, thus increases worldwide warming and climate change. The sector has had allegations raised over its dependence on oil, deforestation practices and loss of forested lands for use in the production of electricity. Coca-Cola proclamations on carbon neutrality and emission reduction goals definitely caught everyone's attention, but some of the stakeholders pronounced it as not serious enough and asked for tougher climate policies and transparency reporting.

2. Job security, Employment, and Human Rights Problems

- Employee Practices and Supply Chain Management: Coca-cola faces allegations of labor rights violation through its foreign distribution networks that include child labor, labor subjugation, and workplace gaslighting. Was accused them of passing on production to subcontractors with poor standards of labor; insufficient output labor protections and abusive labor practices. Coca-Cola's attempt to find solutions related to the best practice of labor conditions, ethical sourcing based on guiding principles and involvement with audits was not correctly set up, mostly in audits and concerns.

- Human rights violations and social impact: The accusations of Coca-Cola for committing human rights violations in the countries where it operates, involve land grabbing, the displacement of local communities and the attacking of the workers. The business suffered from litigation and resistance from inside and outside its premises saying it is used in human rights abuse by its allies in businesses, security in the bottle industries and officials. Coca-Cola's human rights and due diligence tools, lodging of complaints and intervention attempts have been found wanting by many critics who point to the wide-spread nature of the rights risks that are not effectively curtailed by the policy tools.

3. Consumption Safety

- Sales for children and young people:Sales for children and young people: Coca-Cola's advertising campaigns specially targeted at children and young teenagers often appear to most people to be a bother on the assumption that marketing the product in such a way leads to poor quality products, sugary water and too much glucose intake. The organization is accused of using the advertisement techniques and celebrity endorsement of sponsorship to get street synergy between the audiences. The drink's stand regarding aiding nutritional deficiency but over-saturation and contributing to the public health problem has badly faced criticism from the groups of health advocates, policymakers, as well as personal interest in business and industry.

- Health and Nutrition Information: However, Coca-Cola was in the eye-storm of many negative criticism in terms of the alleged misleading claims on product label, marketing does and beverage composition, like high content of sugar, calories and nutrition deficitIn recent years, PepsiCo has been under fire being accused of being an architect and implementer of greenwashing, most prominently misleading consumers about health benefits of the company's products and downplaying the hazards of sugar consumption, obesity and associated diseases. By actively promoting their sugar-free as well as low-calorie alternatives like Diet Coke and Coca-Cola Zero along with addressing public health concerns like obesity; Coca-Cola has shown its marketing capabilities to create a wide range of healthy drinks.

4. Regulatory and Legal Threats

- Regulatory Compliance and Enforcement: Coca-Cola is facing regulatory issues, fines, and penalizing sites concerning environmental infractions, hard work regulation problems, and customer protection issues in different countries. The corporation has been accused of over-regulation, lobbying influence, and regulatory capture which affects governmental regulation and policy, thus eroding the abilities of the government bodies to protect their citizens. The recent ethical mishaps and legal fights, settlements, and penalties of Coca-Cola have set the tone for the customer of Coke, that it needs to focus on business enterprise governance, compliance and ethical business conduct.

- Litigation and Class Action Lawsuits: The Coca Cola Company has been virtually dragged to court and for the past few years engaged in lawsuits and class movement supporting claims of false advertising, customer responsibility, competitive breaks and human rights abuses. The company has encountered the matters of lawsuits from its clients, competitors, shareholders, and advocacy groups against the company demanding damages, stop order and regulatory action because of the alleged wrongdoing. The techniques of Coca-Cola's prison safety, the agreement of negotiations and the response of family members to the courtroom cases have affected popularity, image of the brand, and economic performance of it.

5. Responses and Mitigation Techniques

- Corporate Reforms and Policy Changes: Coca-cola in its response to public stress, regulatory demands and public scrutiny have undertaken policy reforms, constitutional improvements, and agency restructuring. The organization recently hired a CSR specialist, developed and split pending packages to better fight environmental, social, and governance (ESG) problems. While serving the stakeholders, Coca-Cola has conducted stakeholder consultation and set socio-economic partnerships agreed, to solve the slackening environmental issues.

- Transparency and Reporting: Coca-Cola improvement shows in the appropriateness, disclosure reporting and stakeholder engagement through the annual reviews as well as ESG metrics i. e. sustainability performance and CSR practices. CSR reporting of the company is followed by business agencies based on the global levels, frameworks, and terrific practices. Also, GRI and SASB standards are applied. The business world has observed that Coca-Cola's transparent, responsible, and non-preventive CSR reporting and disclosure earn the gold stars from shoppers, rating agencies, and sustainability rankings.

**Leadership and Management**

The Coca-Cola Company through its entire history has been led by great visionary executives who, through their craftsmanship, have created the course for the global effect of their company. Coca-Cola has managed to start as a simplicity and be one of the global giant templates for many of the people from different nationalities and ethnicities. Coca-Cola as one of the global templates benefited from the management of people with numerous backgrounds, decent data, and leadership styles. This is an in- depth overview of the profiles of senior leaders and managing partners of the enterprise who have left their mark on the industry with the launch of new services, strategies, and legacy products that are within the organization and internationally.

1. John Pemberton: The Researcher and The Entrepreneur

It was John Pemberton, a pharmacist and also an inventor, who first introduced the brand and the product known as Coca-Cola in 1886. Insta nur cyfang yn 1831, daw Pemberton yn grair Coca-Cola ar wee vanlime toward, sears, having koca leaf extract and cola nut extract just as two of the main ingredients. Despite the fact that they had to manage tedious, personal and financial claims, Pemberton's entrepreneurial flair was the spark that made him introduce Coca-Cola to the public for the first time as a fountain drink at Jacob's pharmacy in Atlanta. Douglas Pemberton's, the master behind Coca-Cola's trademark, laid the mark for future success and globalization of the company, showcasing the significance of creativity and resilience.

2. Asa Candler: As the marketing visionary, I am determined to implement a comprehensive and effective marketing strategy that will connect with the right audience, convey the true essence of our products, and ultimately build long-term customer loyalty.

It was Asa G. Candler, a local Atlanta businessman, who served as the turning point in Coca-Cola out of an Atlanta-based local drink to the world-recognized and international beverage brand. The ownership of the Coca-Cola brand finally came to Candler after his purchase of this product from John Pemberton in 1888. He then focused on the development of marketing and distribution strategies to boost the visibility and popularity of this product as well as its availability. He made use of innovative advertising techniques that took the forms of distribution of coupons, product sampling and branding to engage the customers and to emphasize the fact that by purchasing his goods they would earn a living. Whoever thought Coca-Cola embodying the American way of life or manners might have been surprised to learn though that as of today, it has emerged as a global icon whose standard is virtually impossible to rival.

3.  Robert Woodruff: S/he is also a Champion of the social cause; as well as a humanitarian in his/her nature.

The person who is best remembered as "The Boss" i. e. Robert Woodruff had the leadership role as the president of The Coca-Cola Company from 1923 to 1955 and he witnessed this company grow to develop as a global giant. Woodruff undertook frontier roles, like the development of the returnable contour bottle, Coca-Cola's bottling network expansion, and shrewd investments in public advertising and sponsorship. But it was his social consciousness that marked him out, as he supported science, education, health, and the improvement of communities worldwide through his philanthropy and civic engagement. While he has been dead for nearly 100 years, his legacy as an innovator who gave back to society impacts the way that Coca-Cola operates even to date.

4.  Roberto Goizueta: The Organization has a paradigm of global strategic approach towards poverty alleviation.

Robert Goizueta, a person of Cuban-American descent who was occupying the managerial positions of chair and chief executive officer of Coca-Cola Center at that time joined the team and during his over 15 years period of authoritative positions, the company got a complete transformation and qualified its spreed to be a worldwide business. Due to his salesmanship, Coca-Cola went globally and introduced new merchandise classifications while utilizing innovation in packaging and distribution. Goizueta's strategic imagination and determined choice-making navy Coca-Cola to never before success peaks, as a result of which it is now among the most famous, recognized and valuable brands on the planet. Coke became so recognizable worldwide because of a shared organizational culture that generated strategic and innovative approaches to work and contributed to growth through the 21st century.

5.  Muhtar Kent: An Individual Who Guides Others and Facilitates Change.

A turkish-american business man Muhtar Kent was the chairman of The Coca-Cola Company from 2008 to 2017and seemed to be managing this organization through long and turbulent times.
Kent focuses on creating constantly advanced tech by having the waste can be reduced through the "World Without Waste " initiative and promoting "5by20 initiative" in the future during his term of being the CSR

executive director. Last but not the least, he also devoted his efforts to expanding coca-cola's drinks range to satisfy changing consumer choices and the dynamics of the market. Kent's mode of control which is illustrated from the actions he undertakes to use empathy, collaboration and to be agile, has resulted in the company smelling good for long term success in many competitive and fast-paced markets across the world.

The profiles of important leaders and CEOs from Coca-Cola's past are a rich resource that reveals the story of the development and amazing success of the business enterprise, and tells how it achieved and continues to be influential to the international corporations and society. Leadership is a crucial ingredient to the Coca-Cola success story ranging from John Pemberton's entrepreneurial spirit to Muhtar Kent's management asserting Coca-Cola's legacy of innovation, endurance and unparalleled quality output. Their vision, dynamism and commitment are the guiding principles behind Coca-Cola executives whenever difficult scenarios or opportunities appear in the market; thus, their identity as an icon that continues to be loved by the sector is highly assured. With a challenging industrial world as Coca-Cola strives to navigate the challenges, the knowledge of its leaders offers not only suggestions but insight for future innovators and molders.

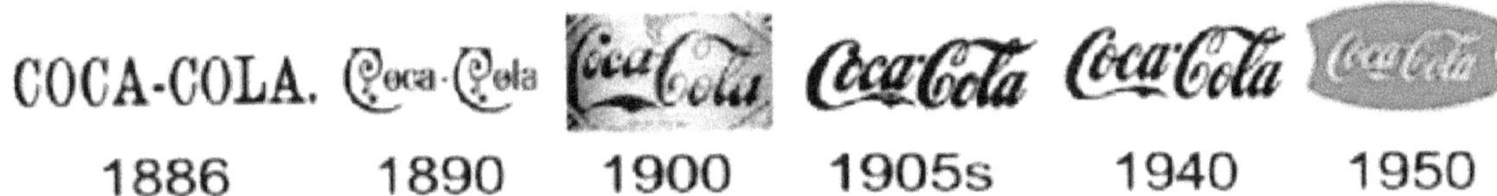

**Future Outlook and Challenges**

The coffee industry is going to undergo dramatic changes due to the mobile users' behavioral changes, market trends movements, and technological progress. This detailed assessment depicts how the modern practices are reshaping the landscape of the beverage sector along with the growing concern for healthy consumption, the rising craving for meaningful drinks, good initiatives towards sustainability, digital transformation, and the impact of COVID-19 on customer behavior and sector dynamics.

The beverage industry is moving to different types of changes which are as a result of changing consumer tastes, societal trends as well as external elements that carry the example of the COVID-19 pandemic. The topic we will focus on today are the key developments and their influence on the sector.

Health-Conscious Consumption:

Health consciousness of consumers engenders the recasting of the beverage world. People are looking for something other than soda drinks with sugars and artificial ingredients. Therefore, this gives more opportunities to the manufacturers that make health products including non-sugar drinks such as herbal teas, sparkling waters and probiotic drinks. This is part of a larger movement toward mindful buying and it features products that contain low sugar levels as well as offer value-adding benefits such as energy and stress relief.

Sustainability Initiatives:

Environment protection has been an acute interest for beverage industry players more and more. The consumer's increasing environmental awareness is pushing producers to adhere to the sustainable practices in the duration of the products lifecycle. It encompasses financing sustainable packaging methods, carbon footprint reduction, and creating reliable recycling programs. Furthermore, there is a phenomenon in the shifting preference from animal-based and natural ingredients towards plant-based and renewable ones as part of their sustainability objectives or being proactive to be in line with consumers' ethical and eco-friendly desires.

Digital Transformation:

Digital transformation is becoming the new normal in any process related to beverages including advertising, customer marketing, and purchasing. E-commerce platforms and direct-to-consumer channels continue to gain significant traction in the market, ushering in new opportunities for brands to achieve direct customer touch and to drive online sales. Successful campaigns make use of digital marketing strategies, influencer participation and personalize promotions for more effective brand interaction and attain high visibility in digital space. The data analytics and the AI-driven insights allow companies to have a clearer view of the consumer behavior pattern, objectives of the marketing campaigns, and product personalization. Thus different nutrition options tailored to the individuals and the subscription services were brought in.

Impact of COVID-19:

The COVID-19 catastrophe has made up for the trend advancement and includes the novel dynamics transformation as well. Electronic commerce adoption picked up driven by a shift towards online shopping and hands-free transactions. Soft drink manufacturers are extraordinarily amping up digital infrastructure development and omnichannel marketing approaches to catch on the market demands and benefit from the e-commerce boom. In addition, historical research has shown that there has been an increasing demand for drinks which can reinforce the immune system as healthiness and wellness have become primary concerns. There are brands that are coming up with products featuring vitamins, antioxidants and ingredients with immune boosting properties to cater to these and also tap into the wide market created by the wellness category.

In a nutshell, these trends envisaged four profound changes in the natural gas and electricity industry. Organizations that harness these changes and discover ways to create value will be the ones who are off course upon this swirling Whitewater and the ones who are more likely to make it through.

### *Coca-Cola's strategies for adapting to hanging market dynamics and emerging opportunities*

As an international beverage enterprise has its own leader Coca-Cola, the company has to face an extremely changing market environment in which customer choices are rapidly changing, new trends are emerging, and technologies are developing very fast. In order to remain on the first place and to take the chances provided by the dynamic market conversion, Coca-Cola approaches a variety of strategies intended to adapt to the context imposed by the dynamic market forces. This analysis including all strategic initiatives of Coca-Cola company becomes the focus of discussion. For example, product diversification, innovation, sustainability efforts, virtual transformation, strategic partnerships, and market expansion are all parts of these strategic initiatives.

Coca-Cola is known for being timely and up-to- date with product diversification, sustainability, digital transformation, strategic partnerships and global expansion, which is how its dynamic approach to staying relevant and competitive in the rapidly changing beverage industry is underlined.

*Product Diversification and Innovation*

Coca-Cola's brand of innovation is also evident in the launch of new beverages and its diagonal variations into non carbonated sectors. Through its never-ending quest to introduce innovative products to the market, Coca-Cola keeps up with modern consumer trends. From health and wellness intentions to energy needs to environmental concerns, this company makes sure to address all demands faced by contemporary society. Coca-Cola's brand products that encompass Coca-Cola Zero Sugar, Diet Coke, Coca-Cola Energy, and SmartWater are witnessing the brand's adaptability to fulfill consumers' various desires.

*Sustainability Initiatives*

Promoting respect for the environment, Coca-Cola is making it a company priority to take action through comprehensive sustainability projects to minimize its negative environmental effects and recover the resources at disposal. The "World Without Waste" concept expressed to water neutrality, reducing the greenhouse gas emission and improving the packaging recyclability conspicuously indicates Coca-Cola's commitment. Promos like PlantBottle demonstrate a mere part of Coca-Cola's responsible sourcing activities and their involvement in the circular economy principles.

*Digital Transformation*

Coca-Cola utilizes technology to make much stronger connections with customers, differentiated marketing operations, and improved supply chain efficiency. Digital platforms, social media, and data analytics become crucial driving Coca-Cola's marketing strategy, the meaning of which is that real time feedback is collected, predictive modeling is performed, and the campaigns are designed to fit a particular consumer's segment.

*Strategic Partnerships and Collaborations*

Working with bottlers, distributors, and foreign alliances which help improve consumers ability to purchase Coca-Cola products. They also allow the company to have better access to marketing insight. Among the strategies used by Coca-Cola to reach and maintain a competitive edge in a fast paced innovative competitive industry terrain, are joint ventures, acquisitions and collaboration with startup companies and venture capital firms to gain access to new markets, invest in new technologies and remaincompetitive.

*Scope of Activity and Mission in Whole World*

Coca-Cola's orientation to select emerging markets and compliance with local preferences confirms that it is a global corporate growth strategy. Uniqueness of product, location-based advertising and cooperation with regional players provide for the successful market implantation as well as the formation of a strong customer loyalty in different cultural realities.

The comprehensive way in the which Coca-Cola company has innovated its products, embraced sustainability, innovated digitally, formed alliances, and expanded globally, is an exhibition of its strength and flexibility in getting through the challenges of the markets and meeting worldwide consumer trends

The Coca-Cola practices of alterations to current market patterns toward growth opportunities demonstrate their advantage as a company in having innovative ideas, sustainability, customer-centricity, and global reach. In addition to broadening its product assortment, promoting by means of digital technology, forging strategic alliances, and sampling sustainability, Coca-Cola can be enabled to maneuverwith the altering beverage market landscape and strengthen profitability and growth. In the context of consumer taste, there is a need for the organization to ceaselessly innovate and remain not only flexible but also able to adapt to changing market trends. This helps the organization to maintain its leadership position and aggressive advantage in the global beverage sector.

### Anticipated challenges and Potential areas of growth for Coca-Cola as a brand

The fact that Coca-Cola keeps on encountering sometimes very difficult situations and at the same time exploiting the existing opportunities, due to its future look, makes its position in the beverage industry very dynamic. This detailed evaluation covers all the possible difficulties Coke may encounter as a logo which need to be thought of, such as changing consumer preferences, reaching market saturation, and so on, also including any interesting trends, technology developments, and geopolitical issues.

However, Coca-Cola has to face up to a set of challenges which seem to be getting tougher and more complicated due to a diversified environment, where people's tastes are changing, regulations are getting stricter, and more competitor brands come on the market. Among the major problems is the changing attitude towards health and wellness among consumers, which indicates a trend of dropping out of sugary beverages and signing up for low sugar alternatives. This trend is a major challenge for Coca-Cola. The company has to invest in the experimental product development as well as innovative marketing strategies with the goal of achieving a fruitful production with low sugar and natural ingredients content.

Moreover, in Caribbean markets like North America and Europe, Coca-Cola has remained at the mercy of these markets' saturation, with per capita consumption of carbonated soft drinks having attained maturity or been on the decline. Keeping the production alive in such a period calls for innovative marketing which should be accompanied by diversifying the product lines and premiumization of some items to compensate at a period where overall sales volumes stagnate.

The restrictions on sugar content and health related taxation and also the adverse effects of health marketing to Coca-Cola brand are considered as challenges in the Coca-Cola business. Governments nation-wide are in the process of implementing initiatives like sugar taxation, labeling, and consumption education for the purpose of reducing obesity and encouraging healthy lifestyles. It comes down to overcoming these amendments, re-formulating products, and claiming the transparent status in labeling are the core tactics for the business to meet these challenges professionally.

The fiercer competition in this niche leads to extra challenges for Coca-Cola. Main opponents include PepsiCo and Dr Pepper Snapple Group which are both fighting for the pie within the beverage industry, together with newcomers trying to break into this industry. Coca-Cola has to put some measures in place to remain competitive; including differentiating its brand, exploring new product ideas, digitization of the existing channels and global distribution of its products.

Another critical area related to the environment is green which is causing even more consumers to be conscious about the pollution with plastics, carbon emissions, and sustainable fashion. Coca-Cola faces the pressure to tackle these issues by choosing eco-friendly packaging solutions, similar to the PlantBottle™ bottles, through launching recycling initiatives and finally reducing its C02 emissions through use of renewable energy and carbon offsetting projects.

Regardless of these facets of challenges, Coca-Cola brand stands many grounds of opportunities that could be tapped. Adding and selecting new consumer markets in the developing countries, going beyond of the carbonated beverages, product innovation, adopting digital technology and e-commerce, and developing strategic partnerships and collaborations are among the most important strategies for the company to cope with the challenges and take the advantage of the opportunities in the soft drink arena which changes rapidly.

Along the path of convoluted drinks business, Coca-Cola faces many issues and decisions necessitated on the mission of breaking new trajectories. On the subject demand of talking retailed choices, saturated market, highly regulated environment the area unit those difficulties that have been predicted in shifting into beverage production, it is the planning for long -lasting revival and success that will make Coke be the best brand. Tap into the potentials of the fastest growing economies of the world with diversification into noncarbonated beverages, innovation in product development, product transformation through virtualization, and strategic partnerships, as a way to hold the position of the market leader in the worldwide beverage marketplace. The future will remain demanding and continue to put pressure on the creation of sustainable longer-term value which will also enable the delivery of shareholder returns, taking into account the evolving needs and acceptable options of global consumers.

## Challenges and Controversies

Coke, as the most international soft drink in the world, has literally been the source of various controversies, health problems, work issues, and environmental crises. However, these controversies haveturned into an all-encompassing consumer trend which is giving rise to ethics conversations in business, among smaller organizations, policymakers, and the media which often mirror the social challenges that many multinational organizations are faced with while trying to pursue more economic goals. These entiretests also study the pros and cons of Coca-Cola, uncovering the reasons, causes, and outcomes of the controversy for stakeholders.

Health Concerns

Coca-Cola the historical past of promoting sugary drinks that increases obesity, diabetes, diabetes, and other he'll problems. The excess amounts of sugar content, as well as the sole dependence on calorie consumption, in their products, have been a major concern to health experts and advocacy groups, hence had asked for stricter regulations, warning labels, and public health campaigns to raise awareness of high sugar intake danger. The use of marketing techniques by Coca-Cola, specified in the audience of children and teens, has subsequently brought unwarranted criticism for their impact on consumption and dietary behavior. The other point is the agencies' push for low-calorie and sugar-free alternatives – the same being proclaimed as healthier options; but, their works are hyped and scrutinized for their efficacy and sincerity.

Labor Issues

Coca-Cola has been accused several times of poor working conditions like child labor, forcing laborers onto showing biases in their international supply chain. Child labor, mismanagement of suppliers and the accuracy level of its producers, have all lost Coca-Cola's reputation resulting in public outrage. In view of the fact that there has been Coca-Cola's operation of how it runs with relaxed labor standards and with no labor protection for the subcontractors, there are questions that arise about its integrity and prudence regarding material sourcing and corporate responsibilities. Furthermore, labor affairs in corporations that are lacking interest in labor rights, union efforts and socio-political justice are always being criticized for putting revenue first.

Environmental Conflict

Coca-Cola's environmental practices, especially in monitoring water consumption, polluting plastic waste, and carbon emissions have provoked anger and protests. The company was accused this year of depleting groundwater resources, spoiling water sources, leaving waste and garbage on beaches, and maritime pollution, environmental degradation and global warming due to carbon production from manufacturing, transportation and refrigeration .

Coca Cola being used as a toilet cleaner controversy:
The statement about Coca-Cola being a bathroom cleaner is a part of an urban tale that has been circulating for so many years. People make an acidic nature guess that coke can dissolve toilet dirt and stains or even deserve to be used as engine-cleaning agent in cars. Nevertheless, there is still no scientific evidence to prove these claims, and Coca-Cola as a company does not encourage or advise their customers to use their product for such purposes. As a result of the molecular aspect, Coca-Cola is an acid due to it being carbonized and containing phosphoric acid. This acidity, on the other hand, provides for the removal of certain substances, but it's not a product that is intended or tested for cleaning of bathrooms and elsewhere. This might be a consequence of using Coke in this way and hence it could pose a threat to surfaces or even have other unintended effects.

On the other hand, the formal position of Coca-Cola company on this matter is, they highlight the fact that their products are designed as beverages to be drunk. They offer tips concerning proper treatment and storage of the products, but they don't advertise offbeat use, like a Coke serving as a substitute for a cleaning agent.

Impacts and Responses:

The controversy around Coca-Cola has been very dramatic driving a lot of cognitive effects on how popular the brand is, how well it performs and relationships with stakeholders. Such as unfavorable publicity, clients not using their services and the monitoring of regulatory bodies, the company has forced them to re-think the way they do business, company regulations, and to give time to the environment. The company has responded to the traumatic situation by undertaking reforms, being more transparent, and engaging with major stakeholders to develop their good practices of coping with their issues. Redefining the negative coverage into beautifying works, lessening the environmental effect, and offering healthier drink alternatives became the goal of the organization which formed the beginning of the effort to counter the backlash these controversies created.

The controversies revolving around Coca-Cola show the wonders of association pastimes, public health, human rights, and environmental sustainability that are linked. In line with the offered example of the global brand of Coca-Cola which operates its enterprise within the beverage industry, the aforementioned organization is confronted with dilemmas related to social, ethical, and environmental issues of its business operations. Despite the fact the business enterprise has attempted to clean itself of such violent controversies and meet its ethical obligations, the continued media glare and condemnation show the necessity of having a strict code of ethics and transparency within companies. Humanizing the working conditions should be Coca-Cola's primary concern because it needs to safeguard the well-being of the workers , communities and the environment to gain favorable public support and retain its leadership position in the society.

### Responses from Coca-Cola and strategies for addressing challenges

In terms of health problems, hardships, environmental conflicts as well as responsibility for and in communities in general Coca-Cola is a very significant company which has many controversies. The Coca-Cola company has deployed an array of measures that focus on reputation improvement and this detailed report exploits the manner in which Coca-Cola answered the conditions required and the strategies successfully met.

*Health Information*

Coca-Cola has been criticized as if it is a drink, which has a lot of sugar in it, therefore, it is related to obesity, diabetes, and many other health problems. In restriction, the marketing department joined the programmes of providing a variety of beverages, specifically those low-calorie and mixed ones. In addition, Coca-Cola has put much effort into creating public health campaigns to educate consumers about a balanced diet, living a healthy lifestyle and embracing personal responsibility. Moreover, the group has been introduced to new cuts of sugar in some products and new products which are healthier as consumer preferences and rules change.

*Labor Issues*:

Charge of the labor rights violations in the Coca cola supply chain led to the board taking a lot of stricter actions, a comprehensive audit and ethical work of the labor practice to be mandatory. Coca-Cola, for instance, has developed a school program for its suppliers and employees working at shift stray sites to increase their concentration on taking accurate measures for enhancement of a safe working environment and to observe working conditions that are realistic. Moreover, the Company has also brought professional bodies, nongovernmental organizations (NGOs), and advocacy groups into contact in order to deal systematically with complaints, disputes and well-being of their workers globally.

*Environmental Conflict*

The use of water by Coca-Cola, including plastic packaging and carbon emissions as concerns play a major role and has publicized the organization Source In response, it sets goals for sustainability, whereby it plans to reduce water consumption and plastic waste, and not be carbon neutral in its operations. Coca Cola has invested in water management services, ties with the community, and technology improvements to minimize the environmental impact and also sustainability of Ez. In addition, the company has sold the cyclic market principles, reduced the package bulky, and used the sustainably manufactured selling materials. Effort is being given in coming up with packaging solutions.

*Stakeholder Engagement*

Coca-Cola Company has realized that stakeholder engagement plays a role of building trust, providing transparency, and making the business known. The NGO has created formal procedures for communicating, listening, and thee contributing to the efforts of stakeholders such as the consumers, clients, staff, suppliers, and society organizations. Researchers s Coca Cola routinely run stakeholder consultations, surveys, and forums to gather the feedback, uncertainty, and insights for surfacing the evolving issues ahead. Furthermore, the company has established professional departments and executives who are in charge of stakeholders' circles comprising the communicators and public-affairs and will coordinate comprehensive communication and networking across various stakeholders.


The following steps and strategies of Coca-Cola company to deal with some environmental challenges despite the annoying conditions demonstrate its commitment in good corporate code, society engagement and sustainable growth. Through a commitment to the health and wellness of people, the adoption of ethical standards, the concern for the environment and community social responsibility, Coca-Cola aims to reflect its company value, to meet stakeholder expectations, as well as to contribute to the achievement of an excellent social outcome. After that, the enterprise should be willing to adhere to its methods, innovate its products, and engage with its stakeholders to get ready for the challenges, leverage the opportunities, and advance a much more sustainable future for generations to come.

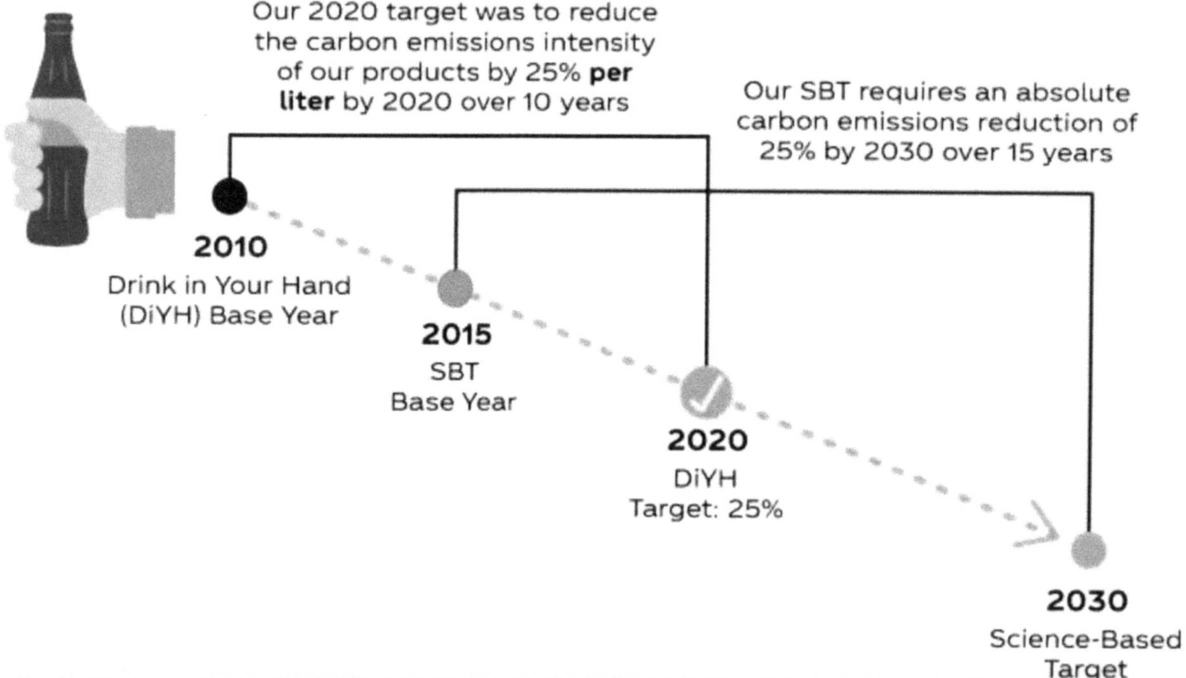


**Impact of controversies on Coca-Cola's brand reputation and consumer trust**

For a brand as long-lived and renowned as Coca-Cola, there is no doubt it's a victim of its own hand's insights and controversies. These controversies can be referred to as health concerns or environmental problems and they had a say on the popularity of the agency in terms of their logo and the same customers were even surprised that they agreed with them. Extensive study, the role of controversies in Coca-Cola's reputation and customer consent as vital, examines thereby, how the company has been negotiating such conflict situations and seeking to seduce the audience again.

*Impact of Controversies on Brand Reputation*

Combined with health claims relating the adverse effects of sweet drinks, some supply chain partners' rights breaches, and environmental issues such as packaging waste and water usage, the controversies over the Coca-Cola brand have been a significant threat to the company's reputation. Coca-Cola has severely suffered by negative media image, social media backlash, and boycotting of consumerism, which has destroyed its reputation as a trustworthy and responsible corporate member. The surveys and studies had shown that these controversies have resulted in the diminishing of the public's minds and loyalties of customers, the necessary step in reputational harm and loss of market share in certain areas.

## Consumer Trust and Perception

Consumer contentment is a huge asset for Coca-Cola as it determines the product choice, brand loyalty and company sustainability. Thus, this company is interested in creating a sense of contentment among the customers. Despite this, troubles began to affect the trust of the customer in the organization's products, prices, quality, sustainability and corporate social responsibility. On the other hand, Loyalty research and brand loyalty survey statistics underline negative sentiments about and representations of Coke, especially among the health-conscious millennials.

## Response strategies and Reputation Management

Coca-Cola has developed a few feedback systems and quality assurance tactics to avoid befalling on the typical conflicts of interest concerning the popular brand name and its intended recipients. This includes the emergency communications, disaster management, stakeholder engagement, and corporate social responsibility services. coca-cola does marketing for traditional and digital media channels to represent the mission, speed, and track record in key topics like sugar reduction, expanded due diligence, and environment advocating for sustainability. The company does multiple responses and seeks people's consent. Even more, they connect with other environmental agencies and institutions like affiliates of the government and NGOs.

## Brand Recovery and Rebuilding Trust

Turning the new page does not mean forgetting and taking guarantee of good standing of the brand forces various Coca-Coca implantation of various measures, such as coping with the root causes, showcasing the real commitment to the responsible business, and recovery of the reputation of the brand. First, the employer came with marketing campaigns, the product improvement that was the customers' responsibilities to ensure winning the hearts and minds of the customers. Coca-Cola has come up with better recipes for its products, environmentally friendly packaging, and cultural or social responsibility programs to reach the changing customer choices and social requirements. However, the organization focuses on transparency and is accountable and has invested morally into the management system is in place to regain its identity as a revered and relied on brand.

The Coca-Cola logo has been viewed by critics as being controversial and controversial, and the people agreeing with this fact have led to the need of a more proactive response strategy and brand management strategy. By turning the focus on matters of importance, connecting with stakeholders, and assigning a high degree of diligence to ethical business operations, Coca- Cola can manage the possibility of controversies, make oral agreements and also guard its time-honored reputations for the future. Going forward, employers must be taking into account possible risks; it has to involve common sense and perception; the product, guidelines, and practices should also continue to be improved according to consumer and societal standards.

**Conclusion**

As Coca-Cola talks its way to destiny, it is confronted with horrible challenges at the global place, while it has limitless opportunities on a world scale. Through adapting digital innovation, sustainability ideas, and customer-related strategies, Coca-Cola can make itself a breakthrough including a brand that speaks the same language with individuals' aspirations and values of today's individuals. Through the policy of careful vendor partnerships, market understanding, and perpetual attention to brand authority, Coca-Cola will take the beverage industry scene and refit the use of the consumers' opportunities in the 21st century and in the times to come.

References

1. Banutu-Gomez, M. (2012). COCA-COLA: International Business Strategy for Globalization. In *The Business & Management Review* (Vols. 3–3, Issue 1). https://d1wqtxts1xzle7.cloudfront.net/59436430/1820190529-118116-pl2ol8-libre.pdf?1559131050=&response-content-disposition=inline%3B+filename%3DCOCA_COLA_International_Business_Strateg.pdf&Expires=1714109954&Signature=Q8DCyZpdLF70vq3acIA2BXFhvz8iJ4gADvo~8HEIZq6GwHh7w6O2~nmExZp0bbgJx6ixMfF7hyyBENZGxDV8e3axC6UbZk6J7rar8Sg-b3IMM~LwNiOLICqxO-li17PdsoxOiVyEp~X2RbrMs56Yh2lOXUftmASUdt9SLtJ2UBf~MelzVagwQv1BBt7Qx2IxQg9VbEFb9d8Tu1qviUbZwWKq8PIqmW~K926dQ1ukAoqPaT38AWuqGkfA1TfpS0kdPxHAMlfowD~ff2srqAJNpzS-rcKVnqs7oYjuqQpRQyQcnKOCLUonFO1YZ4zDb9dhFU-PTU4xt5-4fNEybefMQw_&Key-Pair-Id=APKAJLOHF5GGSLRBV4ZA

2. Coca Cola: A study on the marketing strategies for millennials focusing on India. (2019). In *International Journal of Advanced Research and Development* (Vol. 4, Issue 1, pp. 62–68) [Journal-article]. https://www.multidisciplinaryjournal.net/assets/archives/2019/vol4issue1/4-1-25-458.pdf

3. Chua, J. Y., Kee, D. M. H., Alhamlan, H. A., Lim, P. Y., Lim, Q. Y., Lim, X. Y., & Singh, N. (2020). Challenges and Solutions: a case study of Coca-Cola Company.

*Journal of the Community Development in Asia/Journal of the Community Development in Asia*, 3(2), 43–54. https://doi.org/10.32535/jcda.v3i2.810

4. Vrontis, D., & Sharp, I. (2003). The Strategic Positioning of Coca-Cola in their Global Marketing Operation. *Marketing Review/the Marketing Review*, 3(3), 289–309. https://doi.org/10.1362/146934703322383471

5. The Coca-Cola Company, Baah, S., & Linda Bohaker. (n.d.). *Strategic Management*. https://d1wqtxts1xzle7.cloudfront.net/44703116/strategic_analysis_of_coca-cola_sandra_baah-libre.pdf?1460571577=&response-content-disposition=inline%3B+filename%3DThe_Coca_Cola_Company.pdf&Expires=1710537843&Signature=Dv2P2fRhG2JRslAvmIn-gxkQuFQUtcUoDi76w0UVzr3vYvgcnmzBQVX6H8a~vik~ypJboImMu04VYXS~avC3ltwCM4jeGPnSX-kxEcE9HBw7PbmRCnBgaNyNIXM90KAJKuhkxQP2foHwKePgqnE5B3czLy1eENgmqrfbScv8GNjHBlah1Xl7y-Ro6PoVcxyQy0M9onwIZuI~Fp5io3zL~gqXXLRrWaliAeLxDfy4qXR-~qFZ9F5DsjL0lX4A38To~njYmzitldA5zocJO-A7BrzalUYnPMf4C1jDISNSG0ZpodQT8CLTLmuM90HLB0Ji0Jn3mE2ck7LVIrpDkBXhDg_&Key-Pair-Id=APKAJLOHF5GGSLRBV4ZA

6.  Lee, J. and Maxfield, S. (2015). Doing well by reporting good: Reporting corporate responsibility and corporate performance. *Business and Society Review,* 120(4), 577-606.

7.  Slater, J. S. (2001, January 1). *Collecting Brand loyalty: A comparative analysis of how Coca-Cola and Hallmark use collecting behavior to enhance brand loyalty.* | *Advances in Consumer Research* | *EBSCOHost.* https://openurl.ebsco.com/EPDB%3Agcd%3A9%3A6973241/detailv2?sid=ebsco%3Apli

    nk%3Ascholar&id=ebsco%3Agcd%3A6686429&crl=c

8.  Sultan, K., Akram, S., Abdulhaliq, S., Jamal, D., & Saleem, R. (2019). A strategic approach to the consumer perception of a brand on the basis of brand awareness and brand loyalty. *International Journal of Research in Business and Social Science*, 8(3), 33–44. https://doi.org/10.20525/ijrbs.v8i3.259

9.  *THE REAL THING: "LIFESTYLE" AND "CULTURAL" APPEALS IN TELEVISION ADVERTISING FOR COCA-COLA, 1969-1976 (COMMERCIALS, COKE) - ProQuest.* (n.d.). https://www.proquest.com/openview/1f09435cd14e7506b59112e4d1159322/1?pq-origsite=gscholar&cbl=18750&diss=y

10. Friedman, T. (1992). The world of the world of Coca-Cola. *Communication Research*, 19(5), 642–662. https://doi.org/10.1177/009365092019005005

11. W, C. J. J., Deloria, P. J., Douglas, S. J., & M, V. E. P. (2011). *The Company that Taught the World to Sing: Coca-Cola, Globalization, and the Cultural Politics of Branding in the Twentieth Century.* https://deepblue.lib.umich.edu/handle/2027.42/86471

12. Krengel, A. F. (n.d.). *The perfect balance: combining global and local strategies for effective international public relations.* SURFACE at Syracuse University. https://surface.syr.edu/honors_capstone/88/

13. Dhar, T., Chavas, J., Cotterill, R. W., & Gould, B. W. (2005). An econometric analysis of Brand-Level strategic pricing between Coca-Cola Company and PepsiCo. *Journal of Economics &Amp Management Strategy*, *14*(4), 905–931. https://doi.org/10.1111/j.1530-9134.2005.00087.x

14. Kotnal, J. R. & Assit. Professor & Head, M.com Programme, BLDEA's SBS, Arts & Commerce College for Women, Vijayapur, Karnataka, India. (2017). Strategic Planning & SWOT analysis. In the International *Journal of Advanced Research and Development* (Vol. 2, Issue 6, pp. 60–62). https://www.multidisciplinaryjournal.net/assets/archives/2017/vol2issue6/2-5-301-844.pdf

15. ABBASI, H. (2017). MARKETING STRATEGIES OF COKE: AN OVERVIEW. In *KAAV INTERNATIONAL JOURNAL OF ECONOMICS, COMMERCE & BUSINESS MANAGEMENT* (Vol. 4, Issue 2, pp. 194–199) [Journal-article].

https://d1wqtxts1xzle7.cloudfront.net/56651528/article-1193-libre.pdf?1527241097=&response-content-disposition=inline%3B+filename%3DKAAV_INTERNATIONAL_JOURNAL_OF_ECONOMICS.pdf&Expires=1715502670&Signature=N42WpTI1dgpoj0yhHVuT-Ok0fyom7C1sx7Vf0g3Os-rsnqHyZ6F5WBOwnLjeSKahVMffyTU82NyTvAkTc6YVKzi0BVTpFs8Li0VELoTUda2uAltWm-T7LKftkL7mwt6Lzjh~piljgMT~cA6nJNfGEymnC3YwbuzZuRhBXlri1D3o8MxxzSusIwx4~vK6pWO4mkkvr-UJLHWjm1nCz883DLJyLKnD4HF7rmcSxap39dL8C1qu34trR8lFq9KOGdpgH3637T-03Baq-Oazx2HtA3m~yTaYMDWJOOT3FEln07b~4sOQwq2Q7wwsKKV1TtErIoIXxuTp1~Uu yI-V33rpcA__&Key-Pair-Id=APKAJLOHF5GGSLRBV4ZA

16. Casaqui, V., & Riegel, V. (2016). Management of happiness, production of affects and the spirit of capitalism: international narratives of transformation from Coca-Cola brand. *Journal of International Communication,* *22*(2), 293–314. https://doi.org/10.1080/13216597.2016.1194304

17. Pendergrast, M., & Crawford, R. (2020). Coke and the Coca-Cola company. In *Routledge eBooks* (pp. 11–32). https://doi.org/10.4324/9781351024020-1

18. The invention of Thanksgiving: a ritual of American nationality. (2013). In *Routledge eBooks* (pp. 51–68). https://doi.org/10.4324/9780203951880-12

19. *An examination of the use of culture by Coca-Cola - NORMA@NCI Library*. (n.d.). https://norma.ncirl.ie/5509/

20. Haas, B., & Stein, K. (Eds.). (2020). Gleanings: a journal of First-Year student writing. In B. Haas, K. Stein, & K. D'Souza, *Siena College* (Vol. 11). https://www.siena.edu/files/resources/gleanings-2021-publication.pdf#page=94

21. *Secret Formula*. (n.d.). Google Books. https://books.google.co.in/books?hl=en&lr=&id=3YnvEAAAQBAJ&oi=fnd&pg=PP1&dq=inside+story+coca+cola&ots=RoW6nHL3Vw&sig=0slnY_5SRF83ZeeAEGPZiyv_egM&redir_esc=y#v=onepage&q=inside%20story%20coca%20cola&f=false

22. Uddin, Md. S. (2011). *The Impact of Sensory branding (five senses) on consumer: A Case study on "Coca Cola"* [Master's Thesis]. https://www.diva-portal.org/smash/get/diva2:504446/FULLTEXT01.pdf

23. Econbiz.org. (n.d.). *The Coca Cola brand and Sustainability - Research Repository*. https://eprints.glos.ac.uk/5550/

24. Guo, X., & Wen, M. (2021). Research on Competitive Strategy of Coca-Cola Company. *Advances in Economics, Business and Management Research/Advances in Economics, Business and Management Research*. https://doi.org/10.2991/assehr.k.211209.467

25. Nair, R. K., Reddy, L. S., Verma, P., Pandey, R., Yuwono, S. T., Sin, L. G., Qi, W. Y., Kee, D. M. H., Gee, O. X., Ing, T. W. S., & Yu, T. (2021). The Impact of COVID 19 Towards International Business Strategy: A study of Coca-Cola Company. *International Journal of Accounting and Finance in Asia Pasific*, *4*(2), 73–92. https://doi.org/10.32535/ijafap.v4i2.1116

26. Sarich, R., Zaman, R., & Misra, C. (2015). Discussion and analysis of the marketing strategy of Coke Zero in the US market. In *MERICI* (Vol. 1). https://press.anu.edu.au/downloads/press/n1800/pdf/ch05.pdf

27. Ben-Chioma, A. E., Tamuno-Emine, D. G., Jack, A. S., & Rivers State University of Science and Technology. (2015). Effects of regular coke and coke zero on blood glucose, serum lipid profile and activities of serum aminotransferases in healthy human subjects. *International Journal of Science and Research (IJSR)*, NOV1512031516. https://www.researchgate.net/profile/Davies-Tamuno-Emine/publication/284413977_Effects_of_Regular_Coke_and_Coke_Zero_on_Blood_Glucose_Serum_Lipid_Profile_and_Activities_of_Serum_Aminotransferases_in_Healthy_Human_Subjects/links/5652de7208ae1ef929759b06/Effects-of-Regular-Coke-and-Coke-Zero-on-Blood-Glucose-Serum-Lipid-Profile-and-Activities-of-Serum-Aminotransferases-in-Healthy-Human-Subjects.pdf

28. *Law Journal Library - HeinOnline.org.* (n.d.). https://heinonline.org/HOL/Page?handle=hein.journals/intpl17&div=11&g_sent=1&casa_token=QmJOuPSTLD8AAAAA:vs8IzLR8BMCvioRfZy4oUuGE0-GBDqsbwre3XIzF29miM7D_fmsAbTUjhftKiU0UftSQBB8&collection=journals

29. *coca cola and technology - TopEssayWriting.org Samples.* (n.d.). https://www.topessaywriting.org/samples/coca-cola-and-technology

30. Sheehan, B. & Sergio Zyman, Former Chief Marketing Officer, Coca Cola Inc. (n.d.). *Introducing corporate-guided markets using Diet Coke as an exemplar.* https://d1wqtxts1xzle7.cloudfront.net/50816519/CGM_-_an_introduction-libre.pdf?1481379754=&response-content-disposition=inline%3B+filename%3DIntroducing_corporate_guided_markets_usi.pdf&Expires=1715503611&Signature=X0dk~2ua1VH5ocjed4Sf4W0OoUH8EFzJKmouYXHe1wPkoPQGLuLrqsMTBay9Ci2V59xtj1wptFtBa9XyL4aIkBhCITW7hKf9hfBKIageaNn2~xWuO2eWC4JNNsf0i6s3nZ1kREPU6cYaKnsc9sqmR5InXJGqFoSINUOyhUHaUS-hC0jnpaGC5CXgM5S9fWXThZ5Bb2yKgBxypV1H~tjZ1ROQGqM-RxJ~-xexF1du3jJiJzAsGxB-LM-kc~deL4IA6C-mPsrwiKvvZrR99EKpVOYCHJWaHBHWe9bGXCv0ONQIAE5xOWCyid098IkHfN91CoU9Tr4HSJrY9p-v9UrZ-g_&Key-Pair-Id=APKAJLOHF5GGSLRBV4ZA

31. Olson, K. (n.d.). *The diet cola wars*. UNI ScholarWorks.

    https://scholarworks.uni.edu/draftings/vol9/iss2/5/

32. Hammond, D., Acton, R. B., & Goodman, S. (2021). The impact of health warnings for

    sugar-sweetened beverages on consumer perceptions of advertising. *Public Health*

    *Nutrition, 24*(14), 4737–4749. https://doi.org/10.1017/s1368980021001257

33. Nandi, P., MD. (2023, December 31). *Diet coke exposed: health risks lurking in your can*

    *of diet*. Ask Dr. Nandi | Official Site. https://askdrnandi.com/diet-coke-exposed-health-

    risks-lurking-in-your-can-of-diet/

34. Chorazy, E. (2020). Coke and health. In *Routledge eBooks* (pp. 207–225).

    https://doi.org/10.4324/9781351024020-14